Libra

.ase
.t wa

Renew
..y item
w: anoth

R
.ver
Plea
it

THE LO

)8

D1144982

"The door flew open, in he ran, the great, long, blue-legged scissor-man." (p. 96)

THE KINGFISHER BOOK OF

CHILDREN'S POETRY

SELECTED BY MICHAEL ROSEN

KINGFISHER BOOKS

Kingfisher Books, Grisewood & Dempsey Ltd,
Elsley House, 24–30 Great Titchfield Street,
London W1P 7AD

First published in 1985 by Kingfisher Books

Reprinted 1986, 1987 (twice), 1988, 1989

Copyright © Kingfisher Books Ltd 1985

All rights reserved. No part of this publication may
be reproduced, stored in a retrieval system or
transmitted by any means, electronic, mechanical,
photocopying or otherwise, without the prior permission
of the publisher.

BRITISH LIBRARY CATALOGUING IN PUBLICATION DATA
The Kingfisher book of children's poetry.
1. English poetry
I. Rosen, Michael
821'.008'09282   PR1175.3

ISBN 0–86272–155–5

Editor: Adrian Sington
Line illustrations: Alice Englander
Colour plates: Jonathon Heap (pp 65, 97, 129, 208)
Pauline King (pp 48, 144, 161, 240)
Francis Mosley (frontispiece, pp 80, 176, 193)
George Thompson (pp 16, 33, 112, 225)
Photoset by Waveney Typesetters, Norwich
Colour reproductions by Newsele Litho, Milan
Printed in Yugoslavia

BROMLEY PUBLIC LIBRARIES | AL BEC
CLASS J 821.08
ACC 262286 4
BK
Pe | INVOICE DATE
20 MAR 1989

CONTENTS

INTRODUCTION

For thousands of years, all over the world, people have been thinking thoughts, dreaming dreams and having ideas. And for thousands of years, all over the world people have been trying to trap these thoughts, dreams and ideas before they were forgotten.

How do you trap thoughts, dreams and ideas? You can put them into words and say them, sing them or write them down.

That's what you have in this book: hundreds of thoughts, dreams and ideas trapped in words for you to read, say or sing. Some are very old, some are very new. Some were written in the United States, some were written in Britain and some were written in countries all over the world and then translated into English. Some of the people who wrote them down have become famous while others you couldn't possibly have heard of, because the poem is by a "boy in a playground" or a "woman in a bus line", on the other side of the world.

If there are any that you like here, share them with someone else. Read them out loud; get a friend or a parent and read them to each other. Get a tape recorder and read your favorite ones on to a tape. Make these thoughts, dreams and ideas live for you as they did once for the people who thought them . . .

. . . have a good time.

Michael Rosen

MAMA DOT LEARNS TO FLY

Mama Dot watched reels of film
of inventor after inventor trying to fly

She is so old she's a spectator in some

Seeing them leap off bridges straight
into rivers or burn their backsides
with rockets strapped to their backs

Or flap about with huge wings
only to raise a whole heap of dust

Or to risk life and limb by leaping off
towers, cliffs, mountains even

Makes her cringe however much she admires
their misguided conviction

Right then she wants to see a relative
in Africa, half-way across the planet

An ancestor

Her equipment's straightforward:
just to sit or lie in a quiet, comfortable
room to find herself there in moments

Is all . . .

FREDERICK d'AGUIAR

THE CANE

The teacher
had some thin springy sticks
for making kites.

Reminds me
of the old days, he said;
and swished one.

The children
near his desk laughed nervously,
and pushed closer.

A cheeky girl
held out her cheeky hand.
Go on, Sir!

said her friends.
Give her the stick, she's always
playing up!

The teacher
paused, then did as he was told.
Just a tap.

Oh, Sir!
We're going to tell on you,
The children said.

Other children
left their seats and crowded round
the teacher's desk.

Other hands
went out. Making kites was soon
forgotten.

My turn next!
He's had one go already!
That's not fair!

Soon the teacher,
to save himself from the crush,
called a halt.

(It was
either that or use the cane
for real.)

Reluctantly,
the children did as they were told
and sat down.

If you behave
yourselves, the teacher said,
I'll cane you later.

ALLAN AHLBERG

SMALL AIRCRAFT

As if I didn't have enough
Bothering me, now I'm confused
By dreaming nightly
Of small airplanes. I don't understand it.

The planes don't care that I dream of them:
Now like chickens they peck seed
From my hand. Now like termites
They live in the walls of my house.

Or else they poke me
With their dumb noses: little fish
Move like this to a child's foot,
Tickling, making their feet laugh.

Sometimes they push and bump each other
Around my fire, blinded by the light.
They won't let me read and the noise
Of their wings excites me.

They have another trick: they come
To me like children in tears
And sit in my lap,
Crying, *Take us in your arms*.

You can drive them away, but they're right back,
Flying out of the polished darkness,
Looking from their eyes like sad dachshunds
As their long bodies float by.

BELLA AKHMADULINA
(translated by Daniel Halpern)

WASPS

Wasps like coffee.
Syrup.
Tea.
Coca-Cola.
Butter.
Me.

DOROTHY ALDIS

THE NIGHT

My eye cried and woke me.
The night was pain.

AL-KHANSA
(translated by Willis Barnstone)

THAT'S ME

Everything that happened that morning is so clear to me,
Although it was all three months ago.
"Will you be all right mum – you don't seem well?"
"Yes, off to school like a good girl."
But I don't understand decimals this morning,
I don't want to change my library book,
   and yet I love reading.
Must I go to the swimming baths this afternoon?
Although I know I'm nearly ready for my green braid.
   I want to go *home*.
The four o'clock bell,
I race up the road until my breath heaves in my throat.
Near home I dawdle, linger, drag –
I can hear my own heart
   and my own footsteps.
A rush of speed up the path –
   a dash at the door –
Dad's smiling face meets me,
His laughing voice tells me I have a new brother.
"You're the eldest, you choose his name."

The eldest! the big sister!
   That's ME.

JULIE ANDREWS

LORD BATEMAN

Lord Bateman was a noble lord,
A noble lord of high degree,
He shipped himself on board a ship,
Some foreign countries to go and see.

He sailèd east, he sailèd west,
He sailèd into proud Turkey,
Where he was taken and put in prison
Until he of life was quite weary.

And in this prison there growed a tree,
It growed so stout, it growed so strong.
He was chained up all by the middle,
Until his life was almost done.

This Turk he had one only daughter,
The fairest creature that ever you see,
She stole the keys of her father's prison
And swore Lord Bateman she would set free.

"Have you got lands, have you got livings,
Or dost Northumberland belong to thee?
What will you give to a fair young lady
If out of prison she'll set you free?"

"Yes, I've got lands and I've got livings
And half Northumberland belongs to me,
And I'll give it all to a fair young lady
If out of prison she will set me free."

She took him to her father's cellar
And give to him the best of wine,
And every health that she drinked unto him:
"I wish, Lord Bateman, that you were mine.

"Seven long years we will make a vow,
And seven long years we will keep it strong:
If you will wed with no other woman,
I will never wed with no other man."

She took him to her father's harbour
And give to him a ship of fame.
"Farewell, farewell to you, Lord Bateman,
I'm afraid I never shall see you again."

Now seven long years is a-gone and past,
And fourteen days well known to me.
She packed up all her gay clothing
And swore Lord Bateman she'd go and see.

And when she came to Lord Bateman's castle
So boldly how she did ring the bell.
"Who's there, who's there?" cried the proud young porter,
"Who's there, who's there? come quickly tell."

"Oh is this called Lord Bateman's castle,
Oh is his lordship here within?"
"Oh yes, oh yes," cries the proud young porter,
"He has just now taken his young bride in."

"You tell him to send me a slice of bread
And a bottle of the best of the wine,
And not forgetting that fair young lady
That did release him when he was close confined."

Away, away went this proud young porter,
Away, away, away went he,
Until he came to Lord Bateman's chamber,
Down on his bended knees he fell.

"What news, what news, my proud young porter,
What news, what news has thou brought to me?"
"There is the fairest of all young ladies
That ever my two eyes did see.

"She has got rings on every finger,
Round one of them she have got three.
She have gold enough around her middle
To buy Northumberland that belongs to thee.

"She tells you to send her a slice of bread
And a bottle of the best of wine
And not forgetting that fair young lady
That did release you when you were close confined."

Lord Bateman then in a passion flew,
He broke his sword in splinters three,
Saying, "I will give you all my father's riches
And if Sophia have a-crossed the sea."

Oh then up spoke this young bride's mother
Who was never heard to speak so free,
Saying, "You'll not forget my only daughter
For if Sophia have a-crossed the sea."

"I only made a bride of your daughter,
She's neither the better nor worse for me.
She came to me on a horse and saddle,
She may go back in a coach and three."

Lord Bateman prepared for another marriage,
So both their hearts so full of glee.
"I will range no more to foreign countries
Now since Sophia have a-crossed the sea."

ALL NIGHT BY THE ROSE

All night by the rose, rose
all night by the rose I lay
I dared not steal that rose
and yet I took that rose away

(translated from Middle English by Michael Rosen)

YOU

You are like the hungry cat
that wants to have fish
He won't wet his claws

(translated from Middle English by Michael Rosen)

I'D RATHER

I'd rather drink muddy water, sleep in a hollow log,
than stay in this town, treated like a dirty dog.

"What news, what news, my proud young porter, what news, what news has thou brought to me?" (p. 15)

THE DEATH OF ROMEO AND JULIET

Romeo rode to the sepulchre, 'mong dead folks, bats, and creepers;
And swallowed down the burning dose – when Juliet oped her peepers.
"Are you alive? Or is't your ghost? Speak quick, before I go."
"Alive!" she cried, "and kicking too; art thou my Romeo?"
"It is your Romeo, my faded little blossum;
O Juliet! is it possible that you were acting possum?"
"I was indeed; now let's go home; pa's spite will have abated;
What ails you, love, you stagger so; are you intoxicated?"
"No, no, my duck; I took some stuff that caused a little fit;"
He struggled hard to tell her all, but couldn't, so he quit.
In shorter time than't takes a lamb to wag his tail, or jump,
Poor Romeo was stiff and pale as any whitewashed pump.
Then Juliet seized that awful knife, and in her bosom stuck it,
Let out a most terrific yell, fell down, and kicked the bucket.

THE DEVIL IN TEXAS

He scattered tarantulas over the roads,
Put thorns on the cactus and horns on the toads,
He sprinkled the sands with millions of ants
So the man who sits down must wear soles on his pants.
He lengthened the horns of the Texas steer,
And added an inch to the jack rabbit's ear;
He put mouths full of teeth in all of the lakes,
And under the rocks he put rattlesnakes.

He hung thorns and brambles on all of the trees,
He mixed up the dust with jiggers and fleas;
The rattlesnake bites you, the scorpion stings,
The mosquito delights you by buzzing his wings.
The heat in the summer's a hundred and ten,
Too hot for the Devil and too hot for men;
And all who remain in that climate soon bear
Cuts, bites, and stings, from their feet to their hair.

He quickened the buck of the bronco steed,
And poisoned the feet of the centipede;
The wild boar roams in the black chaparral;
It's a hell of a place that we've got for a hell.
He planted red pepper beside every brook;
The Mexicans use them in all that they cook.
Just dine with a Mexican, then you will shout,
"I've hell on the inside as well as the out!"

A TRIP TO MORROW

I started on a journey just about a week ago
For the little town of Morrow in the State of Ohio.
I never was a traveller and really didn't know
That Morrow had been ridiculed a century or so.
I went down to the depot for my ticket and applied
For tips regarding Morrow, interviewed the station guide.
Said I, "My friend, I want to go to Morrow and return
Not later than to-morrow, for I haven't time to burn."

Said he to me, "Now let me see, if I have heard you right,
You want to go to Morrow and come back to-morrow night,
You should have gone to Morrow yesterday and back to-day,
For if you started yesterday to Morrow, don't you see
You should have got to Morrow and returned to-day at three.
The train that started yesterday, now understand me right,
To-day it gets to Morrow and returns to-morrow night."

"Now if you start to Morrow, you will surely land
To-morrow into Morrow, not to-day you understand,
For the train to-day to Morrow, if the schedule is right
Will get you into Morrow by about to-morrow night."
Said I, "I guess you know it all, but kindly let me say,
How can I go to Morrow if I leave the town to-day?"
Said he, "You cannot go to Morrow any more to-day,
For the train that goes to Morrow is a mile upon its way."

WHAT BECAME OF THEM?

He was a rat, and she was a rat,
    And down in one hole they did dwell,
And both were as black as a witch's cat,
    And they loved one another well.

He had a tail, and she had a tail,
    Both long and curling and fine;
And each said, "Yours is the finest tail
    In the world, excepting mine."

He smelt the cheese, and she smelt the cheese,
    And they both pronounced it good;
And both remarked it would greatly add
    To the charms of their daily food.

So he ventured out, and she ventured out,
    And I saw them go with pain;
But what befell them I never can tell,
    For they never came back again.

GENIUS

On my first birthday I had a brilliant idea.
I was convinced I could do it –
build a robot.
So, the evening of my birthday,
I collected all the things I needed
and at 10 o'clock I started.
I tried not to make any noise
but I did
so my mother and father came in and asked me
what I was doing.
But I was only one
so all I could say was "Mummy, Mummy."
So they left me to get on with my robot.

In the morning I'd finished.
When my Mum came in to dress me,
she fainted with surprise.
My Dad came in and rescued my Mum.
Then they called in some scientists
to examine my robot.
They were amazed at my hard work
and skill.
They called in the press
who took pictures of me and my robot
and wrote the whole story down.
The next day
I'd been seen all over the world in the Daily Dust!
I was so pleased with myself.
In the end
my robot was put on exhibition in the museum
and I was called
The World's First Baby to invent a robot.
When I'm two I shall probably invent something else.

OLD JOE CLARKE

Old Joe Clarke, he had a house,
Was fifteen stories high,
And every darn room in that house
Was full of chicken pie.

I went down to Old Joe Clarke's
And found him eating supper;
I stubbed my toe on the table leg
And stuck my nose in the butter.

I went down to Old Joe Clarke's
But Old Joe wasn't in;
I sat right down on the red-hot stove
And got right up again.

CORK AND WORK AND CARD AND WARD

I take it you already know
Of tough and bough and cough and dough?
Others may stumble, but not you
On hiccough, thorough, laugh, and through?
I write in case you wish perhaps
To learn of less familiar traps:
Beware of heard, a dreadful word
That looks like beard, and sounds like bird.
And dead: it's said like bed, not bead;
For goodness' sake, don't call it "deed"!
Watch out for meat and great and threat
(They rhyme with suite and straight and debt).
A moth is not a moth in mother,
Nor both in bother, broth in brother.
And here is not a match for there,
Nor dear for bear, or fear for pear.
There's dose and rose, there's also lose
(Just look them up), and goose, and choose,
And cork and work, and card and ward,
And font and front, and word and sword,
And do and go and thwart and cart –
Come come, I've barely made a start!
A dreadful language? Man alive,
I'd mastered it when I was five!

NIGHT MAIL

This is the night mail crossing the border,
Bringing the cheque and the postal order,
Letters for the rich, letters for the poor,
The shop at the corner and the girl next door.
Pulling up Beattock, a steady climb –
The gradient's against her, but she's on time.

Past cotton grass and moorland boulder
Shovelling white steam over her shoulder,
Snorting noisily as she passes
Silent miles of wind-bent grasses.

Birds turn their heads as she approaches,
Stare from the bushes at her black-faced coaches.
Sheep-dogs cannot turn her course,
They slumber on with paws across.
In the farm she passes no one wakes,
But a jug in the bedroom gently shakes.

Dawn freshens, the climb is done.
Down towards Glasgow she descends
Towards the steam tugs yelping down the glade of cranes,
Towards the fields of apparatus, the furnaces
Set on the dark plain like gigantic chessmen.
All Scotland waits for her:
In the dark glens, beside the pale-green lochs
Men long for news.

Letters of thanks, letters from banks,
Letters of joy from girl and boy,
Receipted bills and invitations
To inspect new stock or visit relations,
And applications for situations
And timid lovers' declarations
And gossip, gossip from all the nations,
News circumstantial, news financial,
Letters with holiday snaps to enlarge in,
Letters with faces scrawled in the margin,
Letters from uncles, cousins and aunts,
Letters to Scotland from the South of France,
Letters of condolence to Highlands and Lowlands,
Notes from overseas to Hebrides –

Written on paper of every hue,
The pink, the violet, the white and the blue,
The chatty, the catty, the boring, adoring,
The cold and official and the heart outpouring,
Clever, stupid, short and long,
The typed and printed and the spelt all wrong.

Thousands are still asleep
Dreaming of terrifying monsters,
Or of friendly tea beside the band at Cranston's or Crawford's,
Asleep in working Glasgow, asleep in well-set Edinburgh,
Asleep in granite Aberdeen,
They continue their dreams;
And shall wake soon and long for letters,
And none will hear the postman's knock
Without a quickening of the heart,
For who can hear and feel himself forgotten?

W. H. AUDEN

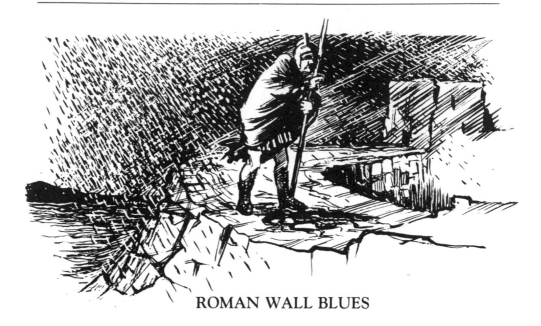

ROMAN WALL BLUES

Over the heather the wet wind blows,
I've lice in my tunic and a cold in my nose.

The rain comes pattering out of the sky.
I'm a Wall soldier, I don't know why.

The mist creeps over the hard grey stone.
My girl's in Tungria; I sleep alone.

Aulus goes hanging around her place,
I don't like his manners, I don't like his face.

Piso's a Christian, he worships a fish;
There'd be no kissing if he had his wish.

She gave me a ring but I diced it away;
I want my girl and I want my pay.

When I'm a veteran with only one eye
I shall do nothing but look at the sky.

W. H. AUDEN

O WHAT IS THAT SOUND

O what is that sound which so thrills the ear
   Down in the valley drumming, drumming?
Only the scarlet soldiers, dear,
   The soldiers coming.

O what is that light I see flashing so clear
   Over the distance brightly, brightly?
Only the sun on their weapons, dear,
   As they step lightly.

O what are they doing with all that gear,
   What are they doing this morning, this morning?
Only the usual manoeuvres, dear,
   Or perhaps a warning.

O why have they left the road down there,
   Why are they suddenly wheeling, wheeling?
Perhaps a change in the orders, dear.
   Why are you kneeling?

O haven't they stopped for the doctor's care,
   Haven't they reined their horses, their horses?
Why, they are none of them wounded, dear,
   None of these forces.

O is it the parson they want, with white hair,
   Is it the parson, is it, is it?
No, they are passing his gateway, dear,
   Without a visit.

O it must be the farmer who lives so near.
   It must be the farmer so cunning, so cunning?
They have passed the farmyard already, dear,
   And now they are running.

O where are you going? Stay with me here!
   Were the vows you swore deceiving, deceiving?
No, I promised to love you, dear,
   But I must be leaving.

O it's broken the lock and splintered the door,
  O it's the gate where they're turning, turning;
Their boots are heavy on the floor
  And their eyes are burning.

                                        W. H. AUDEN

SNAILS

Sound of snails – crying,
Sound drifting through the brush, sound of crying.
Slime of snails, dragging themselves
Along the low-lying plain, crying;
Snails with their slime, crying.
Sound drifting through the bush: dragging themselves along,
    crying,
Snails, their sound blowing overhead from among the bushes.

                            AUSTRALIAN ABORIGINE POEM

WHAT HARM HAS SHE DREAMT

        Her long hair is her pillow
        the girl is sleeping on her hair.
        She cries blood
        she does not cry tears
        she cries blood.
        What is she dreaming?
        what harm is she dreaming?
        Who hurt her?
        who hurt her heart like this?
        Whistle to her, whistle, whistle
        little bird

so she wakes
so she wakes now
whistle whistle
little bird.

AZTEC

DREAM

Once I had a dream that my friend was a carrot and I was a cucumber.
I was never eaten neither was my friend.
We sat in a store ready to be bought.
So one day I ran and ran until I got out of the store. But I forgot about
   my friend.
So I ran back and tried to call my friend
And tell her to come but she couldn't hear me
So I ran back in the store and I almost got stepped on but the lady with
   her shoe kicked me. I fell right back in the carrot pile and I learned
   if you're a fruit don't run away or you'll get eaten anyway.

ILONA BABURKA

I DON'T LIKE MY BROTHER IN THE MORNING

Every morning on a Saturday and Sunday
I go to my paper round at 6.30 a.m.
and by 7.00 I am back home
and I go back to bed to get some sleep.
I make a little bit of noise
when I get into bed,
and just when I am dozing off,
my brother wakes up.
He knows I am awake
and he wants me to stay awake
so he goes outside for a pee –
I know that, because I can hear him
flush the toilet.
Then he bursts inside
and stands in front of the mirror
and says, "SPIDER MAN!!!"

KEITH BALLENTINE

I SAW A SAD MAN IN A FIELD

I saw a sad man in a field
Working,
Each day I ran alongside
Waving.

My father said the man was bad
Wicked,
Forbade me ever more to wave
Friendly.

I walked to school beside the field
Crying,
My friend he understood I felt
Sadly.

He was a German, prisoner
Homesick,
He had a little girl like me
Grieving.

Afraid I walked up to the fence
Gazing,
He smiled and shook his head at me
Smiling.

He was young and blond and nice
Enemy,
I loved him very much indeed
Hurting, hurting.

JOAN BATCHELOR

THE MISTLETOE BOUGH

The mistletoe hung in the castle hall,
The holly branch shone on the old oak wall;
And the baron's retainers were blithe and gay,
And keeping their Christmas holiday.
The baron beheld with a father's pride
His beautiful child, young Lovell's bride;
While she with her bright eyes seem'd to be
The star of the goodly company.

"I'm weary of dancing now;" she cried;
"Here tarry a moment – I'll hide – I'll hide!
[= you are] And, Lovell, be sure thou'rt˙ first to trace
The clue to my secret lurking place."
Away she ran – and her friends began
Each tower to search, and each nook to scan;
And young Lovell cried, "Oh where dost thou hide?
I'm lonesome without thee, my own dear bride."

They sought her that night! and they sought her next day!
And they sought her in vain when a week pass'd away!
In the highest – the lowest – the loneliest spot,
Young Lovell sought wildly – but found her not.
And years flew by, and their grief at last
Was told as a sorrowful tale long past;
And when Lovell appeared, the children cried,
"See! the old man weeps for his fairy bride."

At length an oak chest, that had long lain hid,
Was found in the castle – they raised the lid –
And a skeleton form lay mouldering there,
In the bridal wreath of that lady fair!
Oh! sad was her fate! – in sportive jest
She hid from her lord in the old oak chest.
It closed with a spring! – and, dreadful doom,
The bride lay clasp'd in her living tomb!

THOMAS HAYNES BAYLY

"His favorite little song was 'Make these lubbers walk the plank!'" (p. 35)

TARANTELLA*

Do you remember an Inn,
Miranda?
Do you remember an Inn?
And the tedding and the spreading
Of the straw for a bedding,
And the fleas that tease in the High Pyrenees,
And the wine that tasted of the tar?
And the cheers and the jeers of the young muleteers
(Under the vine of the dark verandah)?
Do you remember an Inn, Miranda,
Do you remember an Inn?

And the cheers and the jeers of the young muleteers
Who hadn't got a penny,
And who weren't paying any,
And the hammer at the doors and the Din?
And the Hip! Hop! Hap!
Of the clap
Of the hands to the twirl and the swirl
Of the girl gone chancing,
Glancing,
Dancing,
Backing and advancing,
Snapping of the clapper to the spin
Out and in –
And the Ting, Tong, Tang of the Guitar!
Do you remember an Inn,
Miranda?
Do you remember an Inn?

* An Italian dance in 6/8 time.

Never more;
Miranda,
Never more.
Only the high peaks hoar:
And Aragon a torrent at the door.
No sound
In the walls of the Halls where falls
The tread
Of the feet of the dead to the ground
No sound:
But the boom
Of the far Waterfall like Doom.

HILAIRE BELLOC

CAPTAIN KIDD
1650?–1701

This person in the gaudy clothes
Is worthy Captain Kidd.
They say he never buried gold
I think, perhaps, he did.

They say it's all a story that
His favorite little song
Was "Make these lubbers walk the plank!"
I think, perhaps, they're wrong.

They say he never pirated
Beneath the Skull-and-Bones.
He merely traveled for his health
And spoke in soothing tones.
In fact, you'll read in nearly all
The newer history books
That he was mild as cottage cheese
— But I don't like his looks!

ROSEMARY AND STEPHEN VINCENT BENET

ON A PORTRAIT OF A DEAF MAN*

The kind old face, the egg-shaped head,
    The tie, discreetly loud,
The loosely fitting shooting clothes,
    A closely fitting shroud.

He liked Old City dining-rooms,
    Potatoes in their skin,
But now his mouth is wide to let
    The London clay come in.

He took me on long silent walks
    In country lanes when young,
He knew the name of every bird
    But not the song it sung.

And when he could not hear me speak
    He smiled and looked so wise
That now I do not like to think
    Of maggots in his eyes.

*In his grave.

He liked the rain-washed Cornish air
　　And smell of ploughed-up soil,
He liked a landscape big and bare
　　And painted it in oil.

But least of all he liked that place
　　Which hangs on Highgate Hill
Of soaked Carrara-covered earth
　　For Londoners to fill.

He would have liked to say good-bye,
　　Shake hands with many friends,
In Highgate now his finger-bones
　　Stick through his finger-ends.

You, God, who treat him thus and thus,
　　Say "Save his soul and pray."
You ask me to believe You and
　　I only see decay.

　　　　　　　　　JOHN BETJEMAN

ECCLESIASTES 3, 1–8

To every thing there is a season, and a time
to every purpose under the heaven: a time to
be born, and a time to die; a time to plant,
and a time to pluck up that which is planted;
a time to kill, and a time to heal; a time to
break down, and a time to build up; a time to
weep, and a time to laugh; a time to mourn,
and a time to dance; a time to cast away
stones, and a time to gather stones together; a
time to embrace, and a time to refrain from
embracing; a time to get, and a time to lose; a
time to keep, and a time to cast away; a time
to rend, and a time to sew; a time to keep

silence, and a time to speak; a time to love,
and a time to hate; a time of war, and a time
of peace.

THE BIBLE

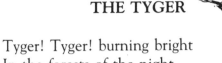

THE TYGER

Tyger! Tyger! burning bright
In the forests of the night,
What immortal hand or eye
Could frame thy fearful symmetry?

In what distant deeps or skies
Burnt the fire of thine eyes?
On what wings dare he aspire?
What the hand dare seize the fire?

And what shoulder, & what art,
Could twist the sinews of thy heart?
And when thy heart began to beat,
What dread hand? & what dread feet?

What the hammer? what the chain?
In what furnace was thy brain?
What the anvil? what dread grasp
Dare its deadly terrors clasp?

When the stars threw down their spears,
And water'd heaven with their tears,
Did he smile his work to see?
Did he who made the Lamb make thee?

Tyger! Tyger! burning bright
In the forests of the night,
What immortal hand or eye,
Dare frame thy fearful symmetry?

WILLIAM BLAKE

COAL FOR MIKE

I have heard that in Ohio
At the beginning of this century
A woman lived in Bidwell
Mary McCoy, widow of a railroad man
Mike McCoy by name, in poverty.

But every night from the thundering trains of the Wheeling Railroad
The brakemen threw a lump of coal
Over the picket fence into the potato patch
Shouting hoarsely in their haste:
For Mike!

And every night when the lump of coal for Mike
Hit the back wall of the shanty
The old woman got up, crept
Drunk with sleep into her dress and hid away the lump of coal
The brakemen's present to Mike, who was dead but
Not forgotten.

The reason why she got up so long before daybreak and hid
Their gifts from the sight of the world was so that
The brakemen should not get into trouble
With the Wheeling Railroad.

This poem is dedicated to the comrades
Of the brakeman Mike McCoy
(Whose lungs were too weak to stand
The coal trains of Ohio)
For comradeship.

BERTOLT BRECHT
(translated by Michael Hamburger)

A MUSICAL INSTRUMENT

What was he doing, the great god Pan,
    Down in the reeds by the river?
Spreading ruin and scattering ban,
Splashing and paddling with hoofs of a goat,
And breaking the golden lilies afloat
    With the dragon-fly on the river.

He tore out a reed, the great god Pan,
    From the deep cool bed of the river;
The limpid waters turbidly ran,
And the broken lilies a-dying lay,
And the dragon-fly had fled away,
    Ere he brought it out of the river.

He cut it short, did the great god Pan,
    (How tall it stood in the river!)
Then drew the pith, like the heart of a man,
Steadily from the outside ring,
And notched the poor dry empty thing
    In holes, as he sat by the river.

"This is the way," laughed the great god Pan
    (Laughed while he sat by the river),
"The only way, since gods began
To make sweet music, they could succeed."
Then, dropping his mouth to a hole in the reed,
    He blew in power by the river.

Sweet, sweet, sweet, O Pan!
    Piercing sweet by the river!
Blinding sweet, O great god Pan!
The sun on the hill forgot to die,
And the lilies revived, and the dragon-fly
    Came back to dream on the river.

Yet half a beast is the great god Pan,
    To laugh as he sits by the river,
Making a poet out of a man.
The true gods sigh for the cost and pain –
For the reed which grows nevermore again
    As a reed with the reeds in the river.

ELIZABETH BARRETT BROWNING

from THE PIED PIPER OF HAMELIN*

Once more he stept into the street;
   And to his lips again
Laid his long pipe of smooth straight cane;
   And ere he blew three notes (such sweet
Soft notes as yet musician's cunning
   Never gave the enraptured air)
There was a rustling that seem'd like a bustling
Of merry crowds justling at pitching and hustling,
Small feet were pattering, wooden shoes clattering,
Little hands clapping, and little tongues chattering,
And, like fowls in a farm-yard when barley is scattering,
Out came the children running.
All the little boys and girls,
With rosy cheeks and flaxen curls,
And sparkling eyes and teeth like pearls,
Tripping and skipping, ran merrily after
The wonderful music with shouting and laughter.

The Mayor was dumb, and the Council stood
As if they were changed into blocks of wood,
Unable to move a step, or cry
To the children merrily skipping by –
And could only follow with the eye
That joyous crowd at the Piper's back.
But how the Mayor was on the rack,

* The Pied Piper charmed all the rats of Hamelin so that they drowned in a river. But he was not paid for doing this so he takes his revenge . . .

And the wretched Council's bosoms beat,
As the Piper turn'd from the High Street
To where the Weser roll'd its waters
Right in the way of their sons and daughters!
However, he turned from south to west,
And to Koppelberg Hill his steps address'd,
And after him the children press'd;
Great was the joy in every breast.

"He never can cross that mighty top!
He's forced to let the piping drop,
And we shall see our children stop!"
When, lo, as they reach'd the mountain's side,
A wondrous portal open'd wide,
As if a cavern was suddenly hollow'd;
And the Piper advanced and the children follow'd,
And when all were in to the very last,
The door in the mountain-side shut fast.
Did I say all? No! one was lame,
And could not dance the whole of the way,
And in after years, if you would blame
His sadness, he was used to say,
"It's dull in our town since my playmates left!
I can't forget that I'm bereft
Of all the pleasant sights they see,
Which the Piper also promised me,
For he led us, he said, to a joyous land,

Joining the town and just at hand,
Where waters gush'd and fruit trees grew,
And flowers put forth a fairer hue,
And everything was strange and new;
The sparrows were brighter than peacocks here,
And the dogs outran our fallow deer,
And honey-bees had lost their stings,
And horses were born with eagles' wings;
And just as I became assured
My lame foot would be speedily cured,
The music stopp'd, and I stood still,
And found myself outside the Hill,
Left alone against my will,
To go now limping as before,
And never hear of that country more!"

ROBERT BROWNING

AFTER PRÉVERT*

We are going to see the rabbit,
We are going to see the rabbit.
Which rabbit, people say?
Which rabbit, ask the children?
Which rabbit?
The only rabbit,
The only rabbit in England,
Sitting behind a barbed-wire fence
Under the floodlights, neon lights,
Sodium lights,
Nibbling grass
On the only patch of grass
In England, in England
(Except the grass by the hoardings
Which doesn't count.)

* Jacques Prévert is a French poet (see *The Eclipse* p. 157).

We are going to see the rabbit
And we must be there on time.

First we shall go by escalator,
Then we shall go by underground,
And then we shall go by motorway
And then by helicopterway
And the last ten yards we shall have to go
On foot.

And now we are going
All the way to see the rabbit,
We are nearly there,
We are longing to see it,
And so is the crowd
Which is here in thousands
With mounted policemen
And big loudspeakers
And bands and banners,
And everyone has come a long way.
But soon we shall see it
Sitting and nibbling
The blades of grass
On the only patch of grass

In – but something has gone wrong!
Why is everyone so angry,
Why is everyone jostling
And slanging and complaining?

The rabbit has gone,
Yes, the rabbit has gone.
He has actually burrowed down into the earth
And made himself a warren, under the earth,
Despite all these people,
And what shall we do?
What *can* we do?

It is all a pity, you must be disappointed,
Go home and do something else for today,
Go home again, go home for today.
For you cannot hear the rabbit under the earth,
Remarking rather sadly to himself, by himself,
As he rests in his warren under the earth:
"It won't be long, they are bound to come,
They are bound to come and find me, even here."

ALAN BROWNJOHN

THE DESTRUCTION OF SENNACHERIB*

The Assyrian came down like the wolf on the fold,
And his cohorts were gleaming in purple and gold;
And the sheen of their spears was like stars on the sea,
When the blue wave rolls nightly on deep Galilee.

Like the leaves of the forest when summer is green,
That host with their banners at sunset were seen;
Like the leaves of the forest when autumn hath blown,
That host on the morrow lay withered and strown.

For the Angel of Death spread his wings on the blast,
And breathed on the face of the foe as he passed;
And the eyes of the sleepers waxed deadly and chill,
And their hearts but once heaved, and for ever grew still!

And there lay the steed with his nostril all wide,
But through it there rolled not the breath of his pride;
And the foam of his gasping lay white on the turf,
And cold as the spray of the rock-beating surf.

And there lay the rider distorted and pale,
With the dew on his brow, and the rust on his mail;
And the tents were all silent, the banners alone,
The lances unlifted, the trumpet unblown.

And the widows of Ashur are loud in their wail,
And the idols are broke in the temple of Baal;
And the might of the Gentile, unsmote by the sword,
Hath melted like snow in the glance of the Lord!

LORD BYRON

Sennacherib was the King of Assyria in the 8th century BC. He destroyed some
cities in the land of Judah whereupon the Angel of the Lord destroyed 185,000
soldiers in Sennacherib's army . . .

THE SUN IS BURNING

The sun is burning in the sky
Strands of cloud are gently drifting by
In the park the dreamy bees
are droning in the flowers among the trees
And the sun burns in the sky

Now the sun is in the west
Little kids lie down to take their rest
And the couples in the park
are holding hands and waiting for the dark
And the sun is in the west

Now the sun is sinking low
Children playing know it's time to go
High above a spot appears
a little blossom blooms and then drops near
And the sun is sinking low

Now the sun has come to earth
Shrouded in a mushroom cloud of death
Death comes in a blinding flash
of hellish heat, and leaves a smear of ash
When the sun has come to earth.

Now the sun has disappeared
All is darkness, anger, pain and fear
Twisted sightless wrecks of men
go groping on their knees and cry in pain
And the sun has disappeared.

IAN CAMPBELL

I HATE AND I LOVE

I hate and I love. And if you ask me how,
I do not know: I only feel it, and I'm torn in two.

CATULLUS

WHAT HAS HAPPENED TO LULU?

What has happened to Lulu, mother?
  What has happened to Lu?
There's nothing in her bed but an old rag-doll
  And by its side a shoe.

Why is her window wide, mother,
  The curtain flapping free,
And only a circle on the dusty shelf
  Where her money-box used to be?

Why do you turn your head, mother,
  And why do the tear-drops fall?
And why do you crumple that note on the fire
  And say it is nothing at all?

I woke to voices late last night,
  I heard an engine roar.
Why do you tell me the things I heard
  Were a dream and nothing more?

I heard somebody cry, mother,
  In anger or in pain,
But now I ask you why, mother,
  You say it was a gust of rain.

Why do you wander about as though
  You don't know what to do?
What has happened to Lulu, mother?
  What has happened to Lu?

CHARLES CAUSLEY

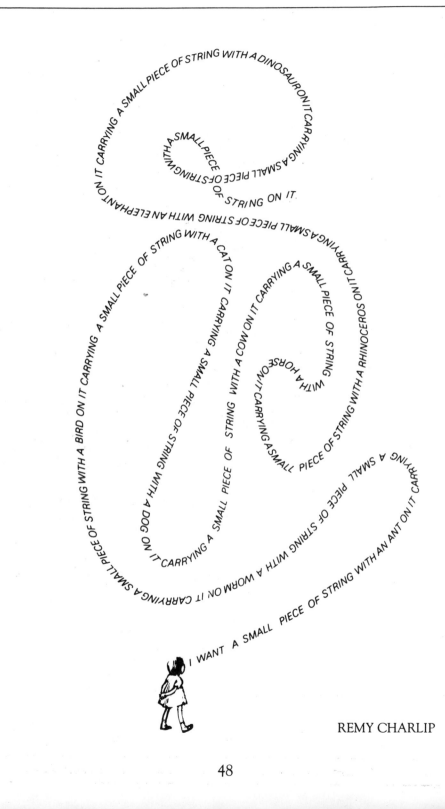

I WANT A SMALL PIECE OF STRING WITH AN ANT ON IT CARRYING A SMALL PIECE OF STRING WITH A WORM ON IT CARRYING A SMALL PIECE OF STRING WITH A DOG ON IT CARRYING A SMALL PIECE OF STRING WITH A BIRD ON IT CARRYING A SMALL PIECE OF STRING WITH A CAT ON IT CARRYING A SMALL PIECE OF STRING WITH A COW ON IT CARRYING A SMALL PIECE OF STRING WITH A HORSE ON IT CARRYING A SMALL PIECE OF STRING WITH A RHINOCEROS ON IT CARRYING A SMALL PIECE OF STRING WITH AN ELEPHANT ON IT CARRYING A SMALL PIECE OF STRING WITH A DINOSAUR ON IT CARRYING A SMALL PIECE OF STRING WITH A SMALL PIECE OF STRING ON IT.

REMY CHARLIP

"He liked to play his bagpipes up and down and that was how he brought us out of town." (p. 49)

THE MILLER
(from *The Canterbury Tales*)

The *Miller* was a chap of sixteen stone,
A great stout fellow big in brawn and bone.
He did well out of them, for he could go
And win the ram at any wrestling show.
Broad, knotty and short-shouldered, he would boast
He could heave any door off hinge and post,
Or take a run and break it with his head.
His beard, like any sow or fox, was red
And broad as well, as though it were a spade;
And, at its very tip, his nose displayed
A wart on which there stood a tuft of hair
Red as the bristles in an old sow's ear.
His nostrils were as black as they were wide,
He had a sword and buckler at his side,
His mighty mouth was like a furnace door.
A wrangler and buffoon, he had a store
Of tavern stories, filthy in the main.
His was a master-hand at stealing grain.
He felt it with his thumb and thus he knew
Its quality and took three times his due –
A thumb of gold, by God, to gauge an oat!
He wore a hood of blue and a white coat.
He liked to play his bagpipes up and down
And that was how he brought us out of town.

GEOFFREY CHAUCER
(translated by Nevill Coghill)

S-T-R-E-T-C-H-I-N-G

Waking up
in the morning
is lovely.
Especially when you s-t-r-e-t-c-h.
You open up
your legs and arms
and stretch.
It's just lovely.
The feeling just makes
you want to do it
over and over again.
But after a while
your stretch
runs out
and it's over.

SHARON CHEEKS

THE DONKEY

When fishes flew and forests walked,
    And figs grew upon thorn,
Some moment when the moon was blood
    Then surely I was born;

With monstrous head and sickening cry
    And ears like errant wings,
The devil's walking parody
    On all four-footed things.

The tattered outlaw of the earth,
    Of ancient crooked will;
Starve, scourge, deride me: I am dumb,
    I keep my secret still.

Fools! For I also had my hour;
    One far fierce hour and sweet:

BROMLEY PUBLIC LIBRARIES

There was a shout about my ears,
And palms before my feet.

G. K. CHESTERTON

THE RED COCKATOO

Sent as a present from Annam –
A red cockatoo.
Coloured like the peach-tree blossom,
Speaking with the speech of men.
And they did to it what is always done
To the learned and eloquent.
They took a cage with stout bars
And shut it up inside.

PO CHÜ-I
(translated by Arthur Waley)

THREE CLERIHEWS

Sir Christopher Wren
Said, "I am going to dine with some men.
"If anyone calls
"Say I am designing St. Paul's."

What I like about Clive
Is that he is no longer alive.
There is a great deal to be said
For being dead.

Daniel Defoe
Lived a long time ago.
He had nothing to do so
He wrote Robinson Crusoe.

EDMUND CLERIHEW BENTLEY

I HAD A BOAT

I had a boat, and the boat had wings;
   And I did dream that we went a flying
Over the heads of queens and kings,
   Over the souls of dead and dying,
Up among the stars and the great white rings,
   And where the Moon on her back is lying.

MARY COLERIDGE

WHAT'S IN A POET'S NOTEBOOK?
(Coleridge goes to The Quantock Hill)

On the tenth day of September
Eighteen hundred Twenty Three
Wednesday morn, and I remember
Ten on the clock the Hour to be.

An air whizzed right across the diameter of
my brain exactly like a Hummel Bee*, Dumbledore,   [Humble Bee]

52

with bands of red and orange plush breeches
close by my ear, at once sharp
and burry, right over the summit of Quantock
at earliest Dawn just between the nightingale that I
stopped to hear in the copse at the foot of
Quantock and the first sky lark that was a song
fountain, dashing up and sparkling to the ear's eye . . .

SAMUEL TAYLOR COLERIDGE

THE DEVIL

From his brimstone bed at the break of day
A walking the Devil is gone
To visit his snug little farm, the earth
And see how his stock goes on.

Over the hill and over the dale,
And he went over the plain,
And backward and forward he switched his long tail
As a gentleman switches his cane.

And how then was the Devil dressed?
Oh! he was in his Sunday's best:
His jacket was red and his breeches were blue
And there was a hole where the tail came through.

SAMUEL TAYLOR COLERIDGE

THE NOSE
(after Gogol)

The nose went away by itself
in the early morning
while its owner was asleep.
It walked along the road
sniffing at everything.

It thought: I have a personality of my own.
Why should I be attached to a body?
I haven't been allowed to flower.
So much of me has been wasted.

And it felt wholly free.
It almost began to dance
The world was so full of scents
it had had no time to notice,

when it was attached to a face
weeping, being blown,
catching all sorts of germs
and changing colour.

But now it was quite at ease
bowling merrily along
like a hoop or a wheel,
a factory packed with scent.

And all would have been well
but that, round about evening,
having no eyes for guides,
it staggered into the path
of a mouth, and it was gobbled
rapidly like a sausage
and chewed by great sour teeth –
and that was how it died.

IAN CRICHTON SMITH

54

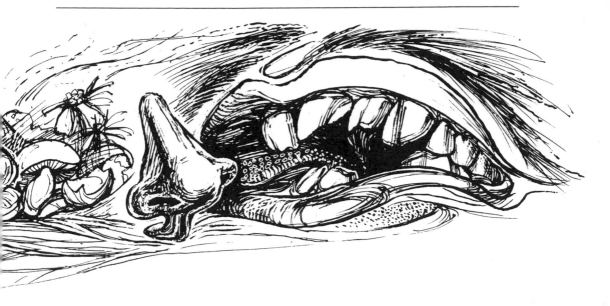

maggie and milly and molly and may

maggie and milly and molly and may
went down to the beach(to play one day)

and maggie discovered a shell that sang
so sweetly she couldn't remember her troubles,and

milly befriended a stranded star
whose rays five languid fingers were;

and molly was chased by a horrible thing
which raced sideways while blowing bubbles:and

may came home with a smooth round stone
as small as a world and as large as alone.

For whatever we lose(like a you or a me)
it's always ourselves we find in the sea

e. e. cummings

Buffalo Bill's

Buffalo Bill's
defunct
     who used to
     ride a watersmooth-silver
              stallion
and break onetwothreefourfive pigeonsjustlikethat
                       Jesus
he was a handsome man
          and what i want to know is
how do you like your blueeyed boy
Mister Death

                 e. e. cummings

THINK CAREFULLY
BEFORE READING THIS

This is a bureaucratic poem.
Please sign (in block capitals)
in triplicate upon receipt.
Knock before entering.
Read the instructions carefully
(Do not exceed the stated dose).
Do not park on the nouns.
Do not walk on the consonants.
Do not spit on the vowels.
Do not recite loudly.
Please leave this poem in the
condition in which you find it.
Flush after use, and
DO NOT DO THAT.

ANDREW DARLINGTON

THE MINER

There are countless tons of rock above his head,
And gases wait in secret corners for a spark;
And his lamp shows dimly in the dust.
His leather belt is warm and moist with sweat,
And he crouches against the hanging coal,
And the pick swings to and fro,
And many beads of salty sweat play about his lips
And trickle down the blackened skin
To the hairy tangle on the chest.
The rats squeak and scamper among the unused props,

[= grows]   And the fungus waxes* strong.

IDRIS DAVIES
(from *Gwalia Deserta*)

SLABBERY FINGERS

My fingers slide down the little calf's throat
Its tongue is rough and pink,
It sucks and slurps
And nearly pulls my fingers off

It slabbers like a baby,
And makes my fingers sticky,
No matter how hard I pull,
It just won't let me go

At last I am free, and look at my fingers,
They are covered in little bubbles
And they nearly make me sick.
The calf puts out his head but I'm away.

FIONA DAVISON

WRITING

and then i saw it
saw it all   all the mess
and blood and evrythink
and mam agenst the kichin dor
the flor all stiky
and the wall all wet
and red an dad besid the kichen draw
i saw it saw it all
an wrot it down an ever word of it is tru

You must take care to write in sentences,
Check your spellings and your paragraphs.
Is this finished? It is rather short.
Perhaps next time you will have more to say.

JAN DEAN

THE BEGGAR'S CURSE

*The Ruffin cly the nab of the Harmanbeck,
If we mawnd Pannan, lap, or Ruff-peck,
Or poplars of yarum: he cuts, bing to the Ruffmans,
Or els he sweares by the light-mans,
To put our stamps in the Harmans,
The ruffian cly the ghost of the Harmanbeck
It we heave a booth we cly the jerk.

THOMAS DEKKER

The devil take the head of the policeman
If we beg for bread, drink or bacon
or milk-porridge, he says: "Be off to the hedges,"
or else he swears in the morning
to put our feet in the stocks
The devil take the ghost of the policeman
If we rob a house we are flogged
(translated by Michael Rosen)

* This is written in the language that thieves used 400 years ago so that other people could not understand them. The translation appears underneath.

PEEPING TOM

I was there – by the curtains
When some men brought a box:
And one at the house of
   Miss Emily knocks:

A low *rat-tat-tat*.
The door opened – and then,
Slowly mounting the steps, stooped
   In the strange men.

Then the door darkly shut,
And I saw their legs pass,
Like an insect's, Miss Emily's
   Window-glass –

Though why all her blinds
Have been hanging so low
These dumb foggy days,
   I don't know.

Yes, only last week
I watched her for hours,
Potting out for the winter her
   Balcony flowers.

And this very Sunday
She mused there a space,
Gazing into the street, with
   The vacantest face:

Then turned her long nose
And looked up at the skies –
One you would not have thought
   Weather-wise!

Yet . . . well, out stepped the men –
One ferrety-fair –
With gentlemen's hats, and
   Whiskers and hair;

And paused in the porch.
Then smooth, solemn, grey,
They climbed to their places,
   And all drove away

In their square varnished carriage,
The horse full of pride,
With a tail like a charger's:
   They all sate outside.

Then the road became quiet:
Her house stiff and staid –
Like a Stage – while you wait
   For the Harlequinade . . .

But what can Miss Emily
Want with a box
So long, narrow, shallow,
   And without any locks?

WALTER DE LA MARE

A BIRD CAME DOWN THE WALK

A Bird came down the Walk –
He did not know I saw –
He bit an Angleworm in halves
And ate the fellow, raw,

And then he drank a Dew
From a convenient Grass –
And then hopped sidewise to the Wall
To let a Beetle pass –

He glanced with rapid eyes
That hurried all around –
They looked like frightened Beads, I thought –
He stirred his Velvet Head

Like one in danger, Cautious,
I offered him a Crumb
And he unrolled his feathers
And rowed him softer home –

Than Oars divide the Ocean,
Too silver for a seam –
Or Butterflies, off Banks of Noon
Leap, plashless as they swim.

EMILY DICKINSON

I'M NOBODY

I'm Nobody! Who are you?
Are you – Nobody – Too?
Then there's a pair of us?
Don't tell! they'd advertise – you know!

How dreary – to be – Somebody!
How public – like a Frog –
To tell one's name – the livelong June –
To an admiring Bog!

EMILY DICKINSON

THE TURKEY

Turkeys don't like Christmas,
which may come as no surprise.
They say why don't human beings
pick on people their own size.
To sit beside potatoes
in an oven can't be fun,
so a Turkey is quite justified
to feel he's being done.

RICHARD DIGANCE

THE BEAR

When the Bear held a Fancy Dress Party,
just about everyone went.
Each animal went as another.
Well, at least that was the intent.

The Bat and Bull went as a Cricket
and the Bison went as a Bath.
The Viper sat on the Hyena's head
and they went as a laughing Giraffe.

The Eagle went as a Birdie
and the Birdie went as a Parr.
(A Parr is an under-aged Salmon,
in case you don't know what they are.)

The Panda turned up like a Penguin,
though he hadn't quite mastered the walk.
No one could tell the difference
when the Butterfly dressed like a Stork.

The Hedgehog turned up as a Buffalo
(Hedgehogs not being that bright),
but everyone said that he'd tried very hard
and he had an enjoyable night.

He almost came second for trying,
but it went to the Hippo instead.
He dressed up as a fairy-tale Unicorn,
with an ice-cream stuck on his head.

The Oyster, disguised as a jewellery box,
sang when his shell opened up.
A good try by Oyster but not good enough
to take home the Fancy Dress Cup.

The Skunk was most unconvincing,
sprinting in like a Gazelle.
It's hard for a Skunk to be anything else,
when they have that distinctive smell.

It was time to declare the Cup winner
and first place went to the Cat,
who covered his tail with red rubber
and hung from a tree like a bat.

RICHARD DIGANCE

A BURNT SHIP

Out of a fired ship, which, by no way
But drowning, could be rescued from the flame,
Some men leap'd forth, and ever as they came
Near the foes' ships, did by their shot decay;
So all were lost, which in the ship were found,
    They in the sea being burnt, they in the burnt ship drown'd.

JOHN DONNE

"They took a cage with stout bars and shut it up inside." (p. 51)

HEAT

O wind, rend open the heat,
cut apart the heat,
rend it to tatters.

Fruit cannot drop
through this thick air –
fruit cannot fall into heat
that presses up and blunts
the points of pears
and rounds the grapes.

Cut through the heat –
plow through it,
turning it on either side
of your path.

HILDA DOOLITTLE (H.D.)

TODAY AND TOMORROW

Happy the man, and happy he alone,
    He who can call today his own;
He who, secure within, can say,
    Tomorrow, do thy worst, for I have lived today.

JOHN DRYDEN

WHO KILLED DAVEY MOORE?

Who killed Davey Moore,
Why an' what's the reason for?

"Not I," says the referee,
"Don't point your finger at me.
I could've stopped it in the eighth
An' maybe kept him from his fate,
But the crowd would've booed, I'm sure,
At not gettin' their money's worth.
It's too bad he had to go,
But there was a pressure on me too, you know.
It wasn't me that made him fall.
No, you can't blame me at all."

Who killed Davey Moore,
Why an' what's the reason for?

"Not us," says the angry crowd,
Whose screams filled the arena loud.
"It's too bad he died that night
But we just like to see a fight.
We didn't mean for him t' meet his death,
We just meant to see some sweat,

There ain't nothing wrong in that.
It wasn't us that made him fall.
No, you can't blame us at all."

Who killed Davey Moore,
Why an' what's the reason for?

"Not me," says his manager,
Puffing on a big cigar.
"It's hard to say, it's hard to tell,
I always thought that he was well.
It's too bad for his wife an' kids he's dead,
But if he was sick, he should've said.
It wasn't me that made him fall.
No, you can't blame me at all."

Who killed Davey Moore,
Why an' what's the reason for?

"Not me," says the gambling man,
With his ticket stub in his hand.

"It wasn't me that knocked him down,
My hands never touched him none.
I didn't commit no ugly sin,
Anyway, I put money on him to win.
It wasn't me that made him fall.
No, you can't blame me at all."

Who killed Davey Moore,
Why an' what's the reason for?

"Not me," says the boxing writer,
Pounding print on his old typewriter,
Sayin' "Boxing ain't to blame,
There's just as much danger in a football game."
Sayin', "Fist fighting is here to stay,
It's just the old American way.
It wasn't me that made him fall.
No, you can't blame me at all."

Who killed Davey Moore,
Why an' what's the reason for?

"Not me," says the man whose fist
Laid him low in a cloud of mist,
Who came here from Cuba's door
Where boxing ain't allowed no more.
"I hit him, yes, it's true,
But that's what I am paid to do.
Don't say 'murder,' don't say 'kill.'
It was destiny, it was God's will."

Who killed Davey Moore,
Why an' what's the reason for?

BOB DYLAN

THE SPACE PROGRAM

People are so bored, bored
Bored
Bored
With
The space program
So that soon
They are going to
Have a shot
And no one
Will show up.
But this is only part of it.
No one will
Be there
When the astronauts come down
On that big Pacific
Ocean.
They will just land,
Starve to death
And sink.
There will end the
Space program.
No one wants
To land,
Starve to death
And
Sink.

WILLIAM EASTLAKE

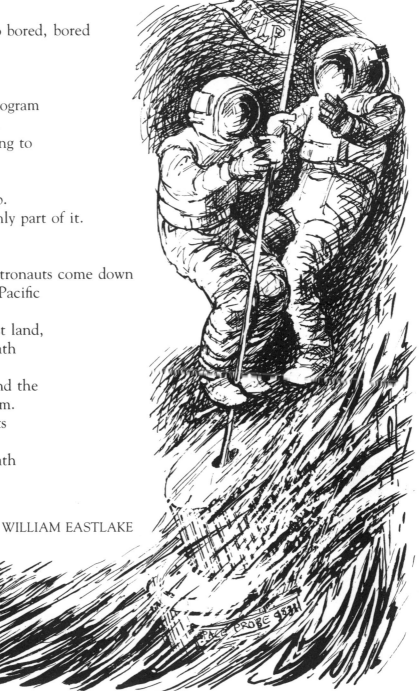

THE LEGEND OF *RA AND ISIS OF ANCIENT EGYPT

Isis wished to become great and powerful,
a maker of things, a goddess of the earth
"Can I not become like Ra?" she asked
And so it was that Isis went to Ra
where he grew old and dribbled and slobbered
and Isis took that spit where it fell to the earth
and kneaded it and shaped it in her hands
till it became the snake.
And it came about that the snake bit Ra
and Ra came to Isis and spoke like this:
"As I went through the Two Lands of Egypt
looking over the world I have created,
something stung me
something, I know not what

is it fire?
is it water?
I am colder than water
I am hotter than fire
my flesh sweats
I shake
what I see, fades in front of me
I can no longer see the sky itself
sweat rushes to my face
as if it were a summer's day"

Then Isis spoke to Ra:
"It is a snake that has bitten you:
a thing, that you, yourself, have created
has reared up its head against you?
I say to you,
it is my power, my words
that will drive out the poison of the snake
I will drive it from your sight
I will put it beyond the reach of the rays of the sun

*Ra is the most important god of Ancient Egypt. Isis is the mother of the gods.

So, godly father,
tell unto me, your secret name,
for if you want to live
it is your secret name that will save you."

and Ra said
"I have made the skies and the earth
I have made the mountains
I have made all that is above them
I have made the great and wide sea
I have made the joys of love
I have stretched out the two horizons
like a curtain
and I have placed the gods there

when I open my eyes
I make light
when I close them
darkness comes.
The waters of the River Nile rise
when I say so
yet the gods themselves do not know
my secret name
I have made the hours

I have made the days
I have made the festivals of the year
I have made the floods of the River Nile
I have made fire
I provide food for the people in their houses

I am called Khepera in the morning
I am called Ra at Midday
I am called Tmu in the evening"

But the poison did not leave the body of Ra
the poison bit into him deeper and deeper
and the great god could walk no more

Then Isis said to Ra
"But you have not said your secret name
Tell it me now
and the poison will flow from your body
for he who tells his secret name
will live."

Now the poison burned like fire
fiercer even than a flame
fiercer even than a furnace
and so the great god said
"I will allow you, Isis
to search into me
so that my secret name can pass from me to you."

Then the great god hid himself
from the other gods
and his place in the Boat of a Million Years was empty

The secret name of the great god, Ra
was taken from him
and Isis the maker of magic
said,
"Poison go!
Flow from Ra now!

It is my magic that moves
It is I
who can make the poison surrender
and flow out on to the earth

Ra live!
Poison die!
Poison die!
Ra live!
These are my words, I am
Isis, the great goddess
the queen of the gods
the one and only
who knows Ra by his secret name."

(From *The Papyrus of Turin* adapted and retold by Michael Rosen)

SKIMBLESHANKS: THE RAILWAY CAT

There's a whisper down the line at 11.39
When the Night Mail's ready to depart,
Saying "Skimble where is Skimble has he gone to hunt the thimble?
We must find him or the train can't start."
All the guards and all the porters and the stationmaster's daughters
They are searching high and low,
Saying "Skimble where is Skimble for unless he's very nimble
Then the Night Mail just can't go."
At 11.42 then the signal's overdue
And the passengers are frantic to a man –
Then Skimble will appear and he'll saunter to the rear:
He's been busy in the luggage van!
    He gives one flash of his glass-green eyes
        And the signal goes 'All Clear!'
    And we're off at last for the northern part
        Of the Northern Hemisphere!

You may say that by and large it is Skimble who's in charge
Of the Sleeping Car Express.
From the driver and the guards to the bagmen playing cards
He will supervise them all, more or less.
Down the corridor he paces and examines all the faces
Of the travellers in the First and in the Third;
He establishes control by a regular patrol
And he'd know at once if anything occurred.
He will watch you without winking and he sees what you are thinking
And it's certain that he doesn't approve
Of hilarity and riot, so the folk are very quiet
When Skimble is about and on the move.
    You can play no pranks with Skimbleshanks!
        He's a Cat that cannot be ignored;
    So nothing goes wrong on the Northern Mail
        When Skimbleshanks is aboard.

Oh it's very pleasant when you have found your little den
With your name written up on the door.
And the berth is very neat with a newly folded sheet
And there's not a speck of dust on the floor.
There is every sort of light – you can make it dark or bright:
There's a button that you turn to make a breeze.
There's a funny little basin you're supposed to wash your face in
And a crank to shut the window if you sneeze.
Then the guard looks in politely and will ask you very brightly
"Do you like your morning tea weak or strong?"
But Skimble's just behind him and was ready to remind him,
For Skimble won't let anything go wrong.
  And when you creep into your cosy berth
    And pull up the counterpane,
  You ought to reflect that it's very nice
  To know that you won't be bothered by mice –
  You can leave all that to the Railway Cat,
    The Cat of the Railway Train!

In the watches of the night he is always fresh and bright;
Every now and then he has a cup of tea
With perhaps a drop of Scotch while he's keeping on the watch,
Only stopping here and there to catch a flea.
You were fast asleep at Crewe and so you never knew
That he was walking up and down the station;
You were sleeping all the while he was busy at Carlisle,
Where he greets the stationmaster with elation.
But you saw him at Dumfries, where he summons the police
If there's anything they ought to know about:
When you get to Gallowgate there you do not have to wait –
For Skimbleshanks will help you to get out!
  He gives you a wave of his long brown tail
    Which says: "I'll see you again!
  You'll meet without fail on the Midnight Mail
    The Cat of the Railway Train."

T. S. ELIOT
(from *Old Possum's Book of Practical Cats*)

75

PRELUDES

The winter evening settles down
With smells of steaks in passageways.
Six o'clock.
The burnt-out ends of smoky days.
And now a gusty shower wraps
The grimy scraps
Of withered leaves about his feet

And newspapers from vacant lots;
The showers beat
On broken blinds and chimney pots,
And at the corner of the street
A lonely cab-horse steams and stamps.
And then the lighting of the lamps.

T. S. ELIOT

HAMATREYA

Bulkeley, Hunt, Willard, Hosmer, Meriam, Flint,
Possessed the land which rendered to their toil
Hay, corn, roots, hemp, flax, apples, wool and wood.
Each of these landlords walked amidst his farm,
Saying, " 'Tis mine, my children's and my name's.
How sweet the west wind sounds in my own trees!
How graceful climb those shadows on my hill!
I fancy these pure waters and the flags
Know me, as does my dog: we sympathize;
And, I affirm, my actions smack of the soil."

Where are these men? Asleep beneath their grounds:
And strangers, fond as they, their furrows plow.
Earth laughs in flowers, to see her boastful boys
Earth-proud, proud of the earth which is not theirs;
Who steer the plow, but cannot steer their feet

Clear of the grave.
They added ridge to valley, brook to pond,
And sighed for all that bounded their domain;
"This suits me for a pasture; that's my park;

We must have clay, lime, gravel, granite-ledge,
And misty lowland, where to go for peat,
The land is well, – lies fairly to the south.
'Tis good, when you have crossed the sea and back,
To find the sitfast acres where you left them."
Ah! the hot owner sees not Death, who adds
Him to his land, a lump of mold the more.

RALPH WALDO EMERSON

THE OLD FIELD

The old field is sad
Now the children have gone home.
They have played with him all afternoon,
Kicking the ball to him, and him
Kicking it back.

77

But now it is growing cold and dark.
He thinks of their warm breath, and their
Feet like little hot-water bottles.
A bit rough, some of them, but still . . .

And now, he thinks, there's not even a dog
To tickle me.
The gates are locked.
The birds don't like this nasty sneaking wind,
And nor does he.

D. J. ENRIGHT

PRIVATE? NO!

Punctuation can make a difference.

Private
No swimming
Allowed

does not mean the same as

Private?
No. Swimming
Allowed.

WILLARD R. ESPY

WHAT'S ITS NAME?

Between my nose and upper lip
There runs a cleft; a trough; a slip;
A runnel; furrow; gutter; split;
I wish I knew the name for it.

WILLARD R. ESPY

WAKING UP

Oh! I have just had such a lovely dream!
And then I woke,
And all the dream went out like kettle-steam,
Or chimney-smoke.

My dream was all about – how funny, though!
I've only just
Dreamed it, and now it has begun to blow
Away like dust.

In it I went – no! in my dream I had –
No, that's not it!
I can't remember, oh, it is *too* bad,
My dream a bit.

But I saw something beautiful, I'm sure –
Then someone spoke,
And then I didn't see it any more,
Because I woke.

ELEANOR FARJEON

SUMMER IN BROOKLYN

Fortune
      has its cookies to give out

which is a good thing

         since it's been a long time since

    that summer in Brooklyn
when they closed off the street
      one hot day
       and the

           FIREMEN

              turned on their hoses
     and all the kids ran out in it

      in the middle of the street

     and there were

         maybe a couple dozen of us

              out there
with the water squirting up
         to the

         sky

          and all over
            us
    there was maybe only six of us
          kids altogether
      running around in our
          barefeet and birthday
   suits
    and I remember Molly but then

"It walked along the road sniffing at everything." (p. 54)

the firemen stopped squirting their hoses
all of a sudden and went
back in
their firehouse
and
started playing pinochle* again   [= type of card game]
just as if nothing
had ever
happened
while I remember Molly
looked at me and

ran in

because I guess really we were the only ones there

LAWRENCE FERLINGHETTI

SOLDIERS

Brother,
I saw you on a muddy road
in France
pass by with your battalion,
rifle at the slope, full marching order,
arm swinging;
and I stood at ease,
folding my hands over my rifle,
with my battalion.
You passed me by, and our eyes met.
We had not seen each other since the days
we climbed the Devon hills together:
our eyes met, startled;
and, because the order was Silence,
we dared not speak.

O face of my friend,
alone distinct of all that company,
you went on, you went on,
into the darkness;
and I sit here at my table,
holding back my tears,
with my jaw set and my teeth clenched,
knowing I shall not be
even so near you as I saw you
in my dream.

F. S. FLINT

SPAGHETTI

A plate heaped high
with spaghetti
all covered with tomato sauce
is just about my favourite meal.
It looks just like
a gigantic heap of:
steaming
            tangled
        mixed
                up
twizzled
                twisted
wound
        up
            woozled
WORMS!
I like picking them up
one at a time;
swallowing them slowly
head first,
until the tail flips
across my cheek
before finally wriggling
down my throat.
But best of all,
when I've finished eating
I go and look in a mirror
because the tomato sauce
smeared around my mouth
makes me look like a clown.

                    FRANK FLYNN

down	and	you	if	find	you	you	will
and	you	love	you	I	love	for	be
up	will	I	love	if	me	love	forgot.
*Read	see	that	me.	And	not	my	

*start here and read up.

SUPERSTINK

Big bus at the bus stop.

Ready to go again.

Big noise.

Big cloud of

ROBERT FROMAN

FRIENDLY WARNING

LISTEN GRASS, TAKE IT EASY. DON'T GROW TOO TALL. THEY'LL JUST BRING IN A LAWN MOWER AND CUT YOU DOWN SHORT.

SEE? I TOLD YOU THEY WOULD.

ROBERT FROMAN

THE ROAD NOT TAKEN

Two roads diverged in a yellow wood,
And sorry I could not travel both
And be one traveler, long I stood
And looked down one as far as I could
To where it bent in the undergrowth;

Then took the other, as just as fair,
And having perhaps the better claim,
Because it was grassy and wanted wear;
Though as for that the passing there
Had worn them really about the same,

And both that morning equally lay
In leaves no step had trodden black.
Oh, I kept the first for another day!
Yet knowing how way leads on to way,
I doubted if I should ever come back.

I shall be telling this with a sigh
Somewhere ages and ages hence:
Two roads diverged in a wood, and I –
I took the one less traveled by,
And that has made all the difference.

ROBERT FROST

LOST

In a terrible fog I once lost my way,
Where I had wandered I could not say,
I found a signpost just by a fence,
But I could not read it, the fog was so dense.
   Slowly but surely, frightened to roam,
   I climbed up the post for my nearest way home,
   Striking a match I turned cold and faint,
   These were the words on it, "Mind the wet paint."

                        JAMES GODDEN

THROWING A TREE

NEW FOREST

The two executioners stalk along over the knolls,
Bearing two axes with heavy heads shining and wide,
And a long limp two-handled saw toothed for cutting great boles,
And so they approach the proud tree that bears the death-mark on its
    side.

Jackets doffed they swing axes and chop away just above ground,
And the chips fly about and lie white on the moss and fallen
      leaves;
Till a broad deep gash in the bark is hewn all the way round,
And one of them tries to hook upward a rope, which at last he achieves.

The saw then begins, till the top of the tall giant shivers:
The shivers are seen to grow greater each cut than before:
They edge out the saw, tug the rope; but the tree only quivers,
And kneeling and sawing again, they step back to try pulling once
      more.

Then, lastly, the living mast sways, further sways: with a shout
Job and Ike rush aside. Reached the end of its long staying powers

The tree crashes downward: it shakes all its neighbours throughout,
And two hundred years' steady growth has been ended in less than two hours.

THOMAS HARDY

THE DOLLS

"Whenever you dress me dolls, mammy,
    Why do you dress them so,
And make them gallant soldiers,
    When never a one I know;
And not as gentle ladies
    With frills and frocks and curls,

88

As people dress the dollies
Of other little girls?"

Ah – why did she not answer: –
"Because your mammy's heed
Is always gallant soldiers,
As well may be, indeed.
One of them was your daddy,
His name I must not tell;
He's not the dad who lives here,
But one I love too well."

THOMAS HARDY

THE THREE TALL MEN

THE FIRST TAPPING

"What's that tapping at night: tack, tack,
In some house in the street at the back?"

"O, 'tis a man who, when he has leisure,
Is making himself a coffin to measure.
He's so very tall that no carpenter
Will make it long enough, he's in fear.
His father's was shockingly short for his limb –
And it made a deep impression on him."

THE SECOND TAPPING

"That tapping has begun again,
Which ceased a year back, or near then?"

"Yes, 'tis the man you heard before
Making his coffin. The first scarce done
His brother died – his only one –
And, being of his own height, or more,
He used it for him; for he was afraid

He'd not get a long enough one quick made.
He's making a second now, to fit
Himself when there shall be need for it.
Carpenters work so by rule of thumb
That they make mistakes when orders come."

THE THIRD TAPPING

"It's strange, but years back, when I was here,
I used to notice a tapping near;
A man was making a coffin at night,
And he made a second, if I am right?
I have heard again the self-same tapping –
Yes, late last night – or was I napping?"

"O no. It's the same man. He made one
Which his brother had; and a second was done –
For himself, as he thought. But lately his son,
As tall as he, died; aye, and as trim,
And his sorrowful father bestowed it on him.
And now the man is making a third,
To be used for himself when he is interred."

"Many years later was brought to me
News that the man had died at sea."

THOMAS HARDY

THE RAILWAY CHILDREN

When we climbed the slopes of the cutting
We were eye-level with the white cups
Of the telegraph poles and the sizzling wires.

Like lovely freehand they curved for miles
East and miles west beyond us, sagging
Under their burden of swallows.

We were small and thought we knew nothing
Worth knowing. We thought words travelled the wires
In the shiny pouches of raindrops,

Each one seeded full with the light
Of the sky, the gleam of the lines, and ourselves
So infinitesimally scaled

We could stream through the eye of a needle.

SEAMUS HEANEY

AUNTIE AND UNCLE

My auntie gives me a colouring book and crayons.
I begin to colour.
After a while she looks over to see what I have done and says
you've gone over the lines
that's what you've done.
What do you think they're there for, ay?
Some kind of statement is it?
Going to be a rebel are we?
I begin to cry.
My uncle gives me a hanky and some blank paper
do your own designs he says
I begin to colour.
When I have done he looks over and tells me they are all very
good.
He is lying,
only some of them are.

JOHN HEGLEY

WHO'D BE A JUGGLER?

Last night, in front of thousands of people,
he placed a pencil on his nose
and balanced a chair upright on it
while he spun a dozen plates behind his back.
Then he slowly stood on his head to read a book
at the same time as he transferred the lot
to the big toe of his left foot.
They said it was impossible.

This morning, in our own kitchen,
I ask him to help with the washing-up –
so he gets up, knocks over a chair,
trips over the cat, swears, drops the tray
and smashes the whole blooming lot!
You wouldn't think it was possible.

CICELY HERBERT

THE SPIDER

How doth the jolly little spider
Wind up such miles of silk inside her?
The explanation seems to be
She does not eat so much as me.

And if I never, never cram
Myself with ginger-bread and jam,
Then maybe I'll have room to hide
A little rope in *my* inside.

Then I shall tie it very tight
Just over the electric light,
And hang head downward from the ceiling –
I wonder if one *minds* the feeling?

Or else I'd tie it to a tree
And let myself into the sea;
But when I wound it up again
I wonder if I'd have a pain?

A. P. HERBERT

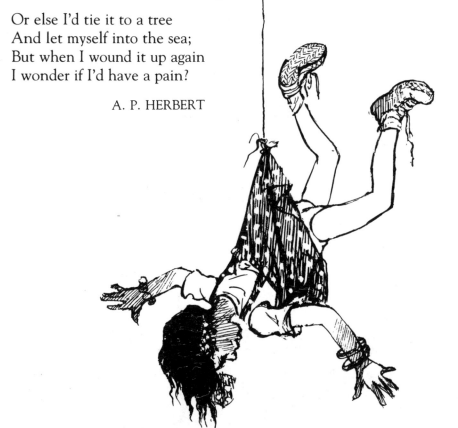

94

IMPOSSIBILITIES TO HIS FRIEND

My faithful friend, if you can see
The Fruit to grow up, or the Tree:
If you can see the colour come
Into the blushing Pear, or Plum:
If you can see the water grow
To cakes of Ice, or flakes of Snow:
If you can see, that drop of rain
Lost in the wild sea, once again:
If you can see, how Dreams do creep
Into the Brain by easy sleep:
Then there is hope that you may see
Her love me once, who now hates me.

ROBERT HERRICK

YELLOW BUTTER

Yellow butter purple jelly red jam black bread

Spread it thick
Say it quick

Yellow butter purple jelly red jam black bread

Spread it thicker
Say it quicker

Yellow butter purple jelly red jam black bread

Now repeat it
While you eat it

Yellow butter purple jelly red jam black bread

Don't talk
With your mouth full!

MARY ANN HOBERMAN

STORY OF LITTLE SUCK-A-THUMB

One day Mamma said "Conrad dear,
I must go out and leave you here.
But mind now, Conrad, what I say,
Don't suck your thumb while I'm away.
The great tall tailor always comes
To little boys who suck their thumbs;
And ere they dream what he's about,
He takes his great sharp scissors out,
And cuts their thumbs clean off – and then,
You know, they never grow again."

Mamma had scarcely turned her back,
The thumb was in, Alack! Alack!
The door flew open, in he ran,
The great, long, blue-legged scissor-man.
Oh! children, see! the tailor's come
And caught out little Suck-a-Thumb.
Snip! Snap! Snip! the scissors go;
And Conrad cries out "Oh! Oh! Oh!"
Snip! Snap! Snip! They go so fast,
That both his thumbs are off at last.

Mamma comes home: there Conrad stands,
And looks quite sad, and shows his hands;
"Ah!" said Mamma, "I knew he'd come
To naughty little Suck-a-Thumb."

DR HEINRICH HOFFMANN
(from *Struwwelpeter*)

"Brother, I saw you on a muddy road in France." (p. 82)

SILENCE

There is a silence where hath been no sound,
   There is a silence where no sound may be,
   In the cold grave – under the deep deep sea,
Or in wide desert where no life is found,
Which hath been mute, and still must sleep profound;
   No voice is hushed – no life treads silently,
   But clouds and cloudy shadows wander free,

That never spoke, over the idle ground:
But in green ruins, in the desolate walls
   Of antique palaces, where Man hath been,
Though the dun˙ fox, or wild hyena, calls,   [= dark brown]
   And owls, that flit continually between,
Shriek to the echo, and the low winds moan,
There the true Silence is, self-conscious and alone.

THOMAS HOOD

In the summer when I go to bed
The sun still streaming overhead
My bed becomes so small and hot
With sheets and pillow in a knot,
And then I lie and try to see
The things I'd really like to be.

I think I'd be a glossy cat
A little plump, but not too fat.
I'd never touch a bird or mouse
I'm much too busy round the house.

And then a fierce and hungry hound
The king of dogs for miles around;
I'd chase the postman just for fun
To see how quickly he could run.

Perhaps I'd be a crocodile
Within the marshes of the Nile
And paddle in the river-bed
With dripping mud-caps on my head.

Or maybe next a mountain goat
With shaggy whiskers at my throat,
Leaping streams and jumping rocks
In stripey pink and purple socks.

Or else I'd be a polar bear
And on an iceberg make my lair;
I'd keep a shop in Baffin Sound
To sell icebergs by the pound.

And then I'd be a wise old frog
Squatting on a sunken log,
I'd teach the fishes lots of games
And how to read and write their names.

An Indian lion then I'd be
And lounge about on my settee;
I'd feed on nothing but bananas
And spend all day in my pyjamas.

I'd like to be a tall giraffe
making lots of people laugh,
I'd do a tap dance in the street
with little bells upon my feet.

And then I'd be a foxy fox
Streaking through the hollyhocks,
Horse or hound would ne'er catch me
I'm a master of disguise, you see.

I think I'd be a chimpanzee
With musical ability,
I'd play a silver clarinet
Or form a Monkey String Quartet.

And then a snake with scales of gold
Guarding hoards of wealth untold,
No thief would dare to steal a pin –
But friends of mine I would let in.

But then before I really know
Just what I'd be or where I'd go
My bed becomes so wide and deep
And all my thoughts are fast asleep.

THOMAS HOOD

STARLINGS

This cold grey winter afternoon
The starlings
On the television aerial
Look like sultanas
On a stalk.

LUCY HOSEGOOD

MADAM AND HER MADAM

I worked for a woman,
She wasn't mean –
But she had a twelve-room
House to clean.

Had to get breakfast,
Dinner, and supper, too –
Then take care of her children
When I got through.

Wash, iron, and scrub,
Walk the dog around –
It was too much,
Nearly broke me down.

I said, Madam,
Can it be
You trying to make a
Pack-horse out of me?

She opened her mouth.
She cried, Oh, no!
You know, Alberta,
I love you so!

I said, Madam,
That may be true –
But I'll be dogged
If I love you!

LANGSTON HUGHES

BROMLEY PUBLIC LIBRARIES

THERE CAME A DAY

There came a day that caught the summer
Wrung its neck
Plucked it
And ate it.

Now what shall I do with the trees?
The day said, the day said.
Strip them bare, strip them bare.
Let's see what is really there.

And what shall I do with the sun?
The day said, the day said.
Roll him away till he's cold and small.
He'll come back rested if he comes back at all.

And what shall I do with the birds?
The day said, the day said.
The birds I've frightened, let them flit,
I'll hang out pork for the brave tomtit.

And what shall I do with the seed?
The day said, the day said.
Bury it deep, see what it's worth.
See if it can stand the earth.

What shall I do with the people?
The day said, the day said.
Stuff them with apple and blackberry pie –
They'll love me then till the day they die.

There came this day and he was autumn.
His mouth was wide
And red as a sunset.
His tail was an icicle.

TED HUGHES

GREEDY DOG

This dog will eat anything.

Apple cores and bacon fat,
Milk you poured out for the cat.
He likes the string that ties the roast
And relishes hot buttered toast.
Hide your chocolates! He's a thief,
He'll even eat your handkerchief.
And if you don't like sudden shocks,
Carefully conceal your socks.
Leave some soup without a lid,
And you'll wish you never did.
When you think he must be full,
You find him gobbling bits of wool,
Orange peel or paper bags,
Dusters and old cleaning rags.

This dog will eat anything,
Except for mushrooms and cucumber.

Now what is wrong with those, I wonder?

JAMES HURLEY

THE PRIEST SPEAKS

I well remember, many years ago
during the War, one day I was at Lundë
when they were holding a recruiting board.
All men were talking of our country's hour
of danger – asking what the future held.
　There, seated at the table, in between
the Bailiff and the Sergeant, was the Captain;
each boy in turn he carefully examined
and then enrolled and took him for a soldier.
The room was packed, and from the green, outside,
we heard the laughter of the waiting lads . . .
　A name was called; another lad stepped up,
pale as the snow along the glacier's edge.
They called him nearer. He approached the table.
He had his right hand bandaged with a cloth.
He gasped and swallowed, fumbling after words
but finding none, despite the Captain's orders.
Then, in conclusion, with his cheeks on fire,
his tongue now faltering, now pouring words,
he mumbled something of a scythe that slipped
and sliced his finger off . . . A silence fell,
some exchanged glances, others pursed their lips,
their silent looks pelted the boy like stones;
and though his eyes were shut, he felt the blows.
At last the Captain rose, an old, grey man,
he spat, showed him the door, and said "Get out!"
　The boy went. Men fell back on either side
so that he ran the gauntlet through their ranks.
He reached the door, and then took to his heels.
Upwards he ran, up through the woods and moorland,
limping and staggering among the rocks
back to his home, high on the mountainside.

HENRIK IBSEN
(from *Peer Gynt* translated by Peter Watts)

DREAM

It's a madman, I said
he will go through my dream
he will come out the other end
yet no one has left
he is still inside.

NANA ISSAIA
(translated by Helle Tzaopoulou Barnstone)

IRRITATING SAYINGS

Isn't it time you thought about bed?
It must be somewhere
You speak to him Harold, he won't listen to me.
Who do you think I am?
You'd better ask your father
It's late enough as it is
Don't eat with your mouth open
In this day and age
Did anybody ask your opinion
I remember when I was a boy
And after all we do for you
You're not talking to your school friends now you know
Why don't you do it the proper way
I'm only trying to tell you
What did I just say
Now, wrap up warm
B.E.D. spells bed
Sit up straight and don't gobble your food
For the five hundredth time
Don't let me ever see you do that again.
Have you made your bed?
Can't you look further than your nose?
No more lip
Have you done your homework?

Because I say so.
Don't come those fancy ways here
Any more and you'll be in bed
My, haven't you grown
Some day I won't be here, then you'll see
A chair's for sitting on
You shouldn't need telling at your age.
Want, want, want, that's all you ever say

(collated by DAVID JACKSON)

ALL FOR AN ICE-CREAM

"Mum, can I have an ice-cream?"
"Go ask your dad."
"Dad, can I have an ice-cream?"
"Go ask your mum."
"But I've just asked her and she told me to ask you."
"Well tell her that I've told you to ask her."
"Mum, dad's just told me to tell you that you've got to tell me if I can have an ice."
"Oh well I suppose you can but go ask your dad for 10p."
"Right."
"Dad, can I have 10p for an ice-cream?"
"I haven't got 10p."
"Oh come on dad you haven't looked yet and oh hurry the van'll go soon."
"Let's have a look then, ah, there you are."
"Thanks dad, Ohh!"
"What's matter now?"
"The van's gone."

KAREN JACKSON

IT MAKES ME FURIOUS!

When I come upon a child
sad, dirty, skinny
it makes me furious!

When I see food
tossed into the garbage
and a poor man poking around in case
it isn't rotten yet
it makes me furious!

When a toothless woman
hunched and old tells me
she's 26
it makes me furious!

When a little old man sleeps
by his final corner
it makes me furious!

When the poor wait
for the rich man to finish his business
to ask him
for last week's salary
it makes me furious!

TERESA de JESÚS

CHARM

The owl is abroad, the bat, and the toad,
   And so is the cat-a-mountayne,
The ant, and the mole sit both in a hole,
   And frog peeps out o'the fountayne;
The dogs, they do bay, and the timbrels' play, [=tambourines]
   The spindle is now a turning;

The moon it is red, and the stars are fled,
But all the sky is a burning:

BEN JONSON
(from *The Masque of Queens*)

MY TEACHER

What's wrong with my teacher?
Does he shout too
                        much?
Does he give you too much
                        homework?
Does he keep you in too
                        long?
Does he actually like
                        you?
Suddenly it dawned on me,
He
    picks
        his
            nose.

DEEPAK KALHA

107

THE BOY WHO RAN AWAY

There was a naughty Boy,
    And a naughty Boy was he,
He ran away to Scotland
    The people for to see –
        Then he found
        That the ground
        Was as hard,
        That a yard
        Was as long,
        That a song
        Was as merry,
        That a cherry
        Was as red –
        That lead
        Was as weighty,
        That fourscore
        Was as eighty,
        That a door
        Was as wooden
        As in England –
So he stood in his shoes
    And he wonder'd,
    He wonder'd,
He stood in his
    Shoes and he wonder'd.

                    JOHN KEATS

ALABAMA

My brethren,
among the legends of my people
it is told how a chief,
leading the remnant of his people,
crossed a great river,
and striking his tipi-stake upon the ground,
exclaimed, "A-la-ba-ma!"
This in our language means
"Here we may rest!"
But he saw not the future.
The white man came:
he and his people could not rest there;
they were driven out,
and in a dark swamp
they were thrust down into the slime
and killed.
The word he so sadly spoke
has given a name to one of the white man's states.
There is no spot under those stars
that now smile upon us,
where the Indian can plant his foot
and sigh "A-la-ba-ma."

KHE-THA-A-HI (EAGLE WING)

THE SANDS OF DEE

"O Mary, go and call the cattle home,
    And call the cattle home,
    And call the cattle home,
    Across the sands of Dee!"
The western wind was wild and dank with foam,
    And all alone went she.

The western tide crept up along the sand,
    And o'er and o'er the sand,
    And round and round the sand,
    As far as eye could see.
The rolling mist came down and hid the land:
    And never home came she.

"Oh! is it weed, or fish, or floating hair –
    A tress of golden hair,
    A drowned maiden's hair,
    Above the nets at sea?
Was never salmon yet that shone so fair
    Among the stakes on Dee."

They rowed her in across the rolling foam,
    The cruel crawling foam,
    The cruel hungry foam,
    To her grave beside the sea:
But still the boatmen hear her call the cattle home
    Across the sands of Dee.

CHARLES KINGSLEY

AFTER THE BATTLE*

"Ravens gnawing
    men's necks
blood spurting
    in the fierce fray

* The battle took place 1200 years ago in Ireland.

hacked flesh
       battle madness
blades in bodies
       acts of war
heroes felled
       hounds cut down
horses mangled
       tunics torn
the earth drinking
       spilt blood"

from THE TÁIN
(translated by Thomas Kinsella)

A SMUGGLER'S SONG

If you wake at midnight, and hear a horse's feet,
Don't go drawing back the blind, or looking in the street.
Them that asks no questions isn't told a lie.
Watch the wall, my darling, while the Gentlemen go by!
     Five and twenty ponies,
     Trotting through the dark –
     Brandy for the Parson,
     'Baccy for the Clerk;
     Laces for a lady, letters for a spy,
And watch the wall, my darling, while the Gentlemen go by!

Running round the woodlump if you chance to find
Little barrels, roped and tarred, all full of brandy-wine,
Don't you shout to come and look, nor use 'em for your play.
Put the brushwood back again – and they'll be gone next day!

If you see a stable-door setting open wide;
If you see a tired horse lying down inside;
If your mother mends a coat cut about and tore;
If the lining's wet and warm – don't you ask no more!

If you meet King George's men, dressed in blue and red,
You be careful what you say, and mindful what is said.
If they call you "pretty maid", and chuck you 'neath the chin,
Don't you tell where no one is, nor yet where no one's been!

Knocks and footsteps round the house – whistles after dark –
You've no call for running out till the house-dogs bark.
Trusty's here, and *Pincher's* here, and see how dumb they lie –
They don't fret to follow when the Gentlemen go by!

If you do as you've been told, 'likely there's a chance,
You'll be give a dainty doll, all the way from France,
With a cap of Valenciennes, and a velvet hood –
A present from the Gentlemen, along o' being good!
  Five and twenty ponies,
  Trotting through the dark –
  Brandy for the Parson,
  'Baccy for the Clerk.
Them that asks no questions isn't told a lie –
Watch the wall, my darling, while the Gentlemen go by!

RUDYARD KIPLING

"If you wake at midnight, and hear a horse's feet, don't go drawing back the blind, or looking in the street." (p. 111)

THROUGH A GLASS EYE, LIGHTLY

In the laboratory waiting room
containing
one television actor with a teary face
trying a contact lens;
two muscular victims of industrial accidents;
several vain women — I was one of them —
came Deborah, four, to pick up her glass eye.

It was a long day:
Deborah waiting for the blood-vessels
painted
on her iris to dry.
Her mother said that, holding Deborah
when she was born,
"First I inspected her, from toes to navel,
then stopped at her head . . ."
We wondered why
the inspection hadn't gone the other way.
"Looking into her eye
was like looking into a volcano:

"Her vacant pupil
went whirling down, down to the foundation
of the world . . .
When she was three months old they took it out.
She giggled when she went under
the anesthetic.
Forty-five minutes later she came back
happy! . . .

The gas wore off, she found the hole in her face
(you know, it never bled?)
stayed happy, even when I went to pieces.
She's five, in June.

113

"Deborah, you get right down
from there, or I'll have to slap!"
Laughing, Deborah climbed into the lap
of one vain lady, who
had been discontented with her own beauty.
Now she held on to Deborah, looked her steadily
in the empty eye.

CAROLYN KIZER

THE JUMBLIES

They went to sea in a Sieve, they did,
    In a Sieve they went to sea:
In spite of all their friends could say,
On a winter's morn, on a stormy day,
    In a Sieve they went to sea!
And when the Sieve turned round and round,
And everyone cried, "You'll all be drowned!"
They called aloud, "Our Sieve ain't big,
But we don't care a button! we don't care a fig!
    In a Sieve we'll go to sea!"
        Far and few, far and few,
           Are the lands where the Jumblies live;
        Their heads are green, and their hands are blue,
           And they went to sea in a Sieve.

They sailed away in a Sieve, they did,
    In a Sieve they sailed so fast,
With only a beautiful pea-green veil
Tied with a riband by way of a sail,
    To a small tobacco-pipe mast;
And everyone said, who saw them go,

114

"O won't they be soon upset, you know!
For the sky is dark, and the voyage is long,
And happen what may, it's extremely wrong
    In a Sieve to sail so fast!"
        Far and few, far and few,
            Are the lands where the Jumblies live;
        Their heads are green, and their hands are blue,
            And they went to sea in a Sieve.

The water it soon came in, it did,
        The water it soon came in;
So to keep them dry, they wrapped their feet
In a pinky paper all folded neat,
        And they fastened it down with a pin.
And they passed the night in a crockery-jar,
And each of them said, "How wise we are!
Though the sky be dark, and the voyage be long,
Yet we never can think we were rash or wrong,
    While round in our Sieve we spin!"
        Far and few, far and few,
            Are the lands where the Jumblies live;
        Their heads are green, and their hands are blue,
            And they went to sea in a Sieve.

And all night long they sailed away;
        And when the sun went down,
They whistled and warbled a moony song
To the echoing sound of a coppery gong,
        In the shade of the mountains brown.
"O Timballo! How happy we are,
When we live in a Sieve and a crockery-jar,
And all night long in the moonlight pale,
We sail away with a pea-green sail,
    In the shade of the mountains brown!"
        Far and few, far and few,
            Are the lands where the Jumblies live;
        Their heads are green, and their hands are blue,
            And they went to sea in a Sieve.

They sailed to the Western Sea, they did,
　To a land all covered with trees,
And they bought an Owl, and a useful Cart,
And a pound of Rice, and a Cranberry Tart,
　And a hive of silvery Bees.
And they bought a Pig, and some green Jack-daws,
And a lovely Monkey with lollipop paws,
And forty bottles of Ring-Bo-Ree,
　　And no end of Stilton Cheese.
　　　Far and few, far and few,
　　　　Are the lands where the Jumblies live;
　　　Their heads are green, and their hands are blue,
　　　　And they went to sea in a Sieve.

And in twenty years they all came back,
　In twenty years or more,
And everyone said, "How tall they've grown!
For they've been to the Lakes, and the Torrible Zone,
　And the hills of the Chankly Bore!"
And they drank their health and gave them a feast
Of dumplings made of beautiful yeast;
And everyone said, "If we only live,
We too will go to sea in a Sieve, –

To the hills of the Chankly Bore!"
　　Far and few, far and few,
　　　Are the lands where the Jumblies live;
　　Their heads are green, and their hands are blue,
　　　And they went to sea in a Sieve.

EDWARD LEAR

I'M ONLY SLEEPING

When I wake up early in the morning,
Lift my head, I'm still yawning.
When I'm in the middle of a dream,
Stay in bed, float up stream,
Please don't wake me, no, don't shake me,
Leave me where I am, I'm only sleeping.
Everybody seems to think I'm lazy.
I don't mind, I think they're crazy
Running everywhere at such a speed,
Till they find there's no need,
Please don't spoil my day, I'm miles away,
And after all, I'm only sleeping.
Keeping an eye on the world going by my window,
Taking my time, lying there and staring at the ceiling,
Waiting for a sleepy feeling.
Please don't spoil my day, I'm miles away,
And after all, I'm only sleeping.
Keeping an eye on the world going by my window,
Taking my time.
When I wake up early in the morning,
Lift my head, I'm still yawning.
When I'm in the middle of a dream,
Staying in bed, float up stream,
Please don't wake me, no, don't shake me,
Leave me where I am, I'm only sleeping.

JOHN LENNON
PAUL McCARTNEY

THE PROVIDER

An
eleven-year-old boy
from Loma Linda, Calif.,
died
last week
of
auto-accident injuries.
Within the day,
his kidneys
were transplanted into two men,
an extract from his spleen
was injected into a leukemia patient,
and
surgeons used
some of his skin
as grafts
for a severely burned woman.
(*Time* – May 10, 1968)

found by JULIUS LESTER

THE LITTLE TURTLE

There was a little turtle.
He lived in a box.
He swam in a puddle.
He climbed on the rocks.

He snapped at a mosquito.
He snapped at a flea.
He snapped at a minnow.
And he snapped at me.

He caught the mosquito.
He caught the flea.
He caught the minnow.
But he didn't catch me.

VACHEL LINDSAY

LONDON AIRPORT

Last night in London Airport
I saw a wooden bin
labelled UNWANTED LITERATURE
IS TO BE PLACED HEREIN.
So I wrote a poem
and popped it in.

CHRISTOPHER LOGUE

119

THE CHILDREN'S HOUR

Between the dark and the daylight,
　　When the night is beginning to lower,
Comes a pause in the day's occupations,
　　That is known as the Children's Hour.

I hear in the chamber above me
　　The patter of little feet,
The sound of a door that is opened,
　　And voices soft and sweet.

From my study I see in the lamplight,
　　Descending the broad hall stair,
Grave Alice, and laughing Allegra,
　　And Edith with golden hair.

A whisper, and then a silence:
　　Yet I know by their merry eyes
They are plotting and planning together
　　To take me by surprise.

A sudden rush from the stairway,
　　A sudden raid from the hall!
By three doors left unguarded
　　They enter my castle wall!

They climb up into my turret
   O'er the arms and back of my chair;
If I try to escape, they surround me;
   They seem to be everywhere.

They almost devour me with kisses,
   Their arms about me entwine,
Till I think of the Bishop of Bingen
   In his Mouse-Tower on the Rhine!

Do you think, O blue-eyed banditti,
   Because you have scaled the wall,
Such an old moustache as I am
   Is not a match for you all!

I have you fast in my fortress,
   And will not let you depart,
But put you down into the dungeon
   In the round-tower of my heart.

And there will I keep you forever,
   Yes, forever and a day,
Till the walls shall crumble to ruin,
   And molder in dust away!

     HENRY WADSWORTH LONGFELLOW

HIAWATHA AND THE KING OF THE FISHES

On the white sand of the bottom
Lay the monster Mishe-Nahma,
Lay the sturgeon, King of Fishes;
Through his gills he breathed the water,
With his fins he fanned and winnowed,
With his tail he swept the sand-floor.

There he lay in all his armor;
On each side a shield to guard him,
Plate of bone upon his forehead,
Down his sides and back and shoulders
Plates of bone with spines projecting!
Painted was he with his war-paints,
Stripes of yellow, red, and azure,
Spots of brown and spots of sable;
And he lay there on the bottom,
Fanning with his fins of purple,
As above him Hiawatha
In his birch-canoe came sailing,
With his fishing-line of cedar.

"Take my bait!" cried Hiawatha,
Down into the depths beneath him.
"Take my bait, O Sturgeon, Nahma!
Come up from below the water,
Let us see which is the stronger!"
And he dropped his line of cedar
Through the clear, transparent water,
Waited vainly for an answer,
Long sat waiting for an answer,
And repeating loud and louder,
"Take my bait, O King of Fishes!"

From the white sand of the bottom
Up he rose with angry gesture,
Quivering in each nerve and fiber,

Clashing all his plates of armor,
Gleaming bright with all his war-paint;
In his wrath he darted upward,
Flashing leaped into the sunshine,
Opened his great jaws, and swallowed
Both canoe and Hiawatha.

Down into that darksome cavern
Plunged the headlong Hiawatha,
As a log on some black river
Shoots and plunges down the rapids,
Found himself in utter darkness,
Groped about in helpless wonder,
Till he felt a great heart beating,
Throbbing in that utter darkness.

And he smote it in his anger
With his fists, the heart of Nahma,
Felt the mighty King of Fishes
Shudder through each nerve and fiber,
Heard the water gurgle round him
As he leaped and staggered through it,
Sick at heart, and faint and weary.

And again the sturgeon, Nahma,
Gasped and quivered in the water,
Then was still, and drifted landward
Till he grated on the pebbles,
Till the listening Hiawatha
Heard him grate upon the margin,
Felt him strand upon the pebbles,
Knew that Nahma, King of Fishes,
Lay there dead upon the margin.

Then he heard a clang and flapping,
As of many wings assembling,
Heard a screaming and confusion,
As of birds of prey contending,
Saw a gleam of light above him,
Shining through the ribs of Nahma,
Saw the glittering eyes of sea-gulls
Of Kayoshk, the sea-gulls, peering,
Gazing at him through the opening,
Heard them saying to each other,
" 'Tis our brother, Hiawatha!"

And he shouted from below them,
Cried exulting from the caverns,
"O ye sea-gulls! O my brothers!
I have slain the sturgeon, Nahma;
Make the rifts a little larger,
With your claws the openings widen,
Set me free from this dark prison,
And henceforward and for ever
Men shall speak of your achievements,
Calling you Kayoshk, the sea-gulls,
Yes, Kayoshk, the Noble Scratchers!"

And the wild and clamorous sea-gulls
Toiled with beak and claws together,
Made the rifts and openings wider
In the mighty ribs of Nahma,

And from peril and from prison,
From the body of the sturgeon,
From the peril of the water,
Was released my Hiawatha.

HENRY WADSWORTH LONGFELLOW
(from *The Song of Hiawatha*)

NIGHT CLOUDS

The white mares of the moon rush along the sky
Beating their golden hoofs upon the glass Heavens;
The white mares of the moon are all standing on their hind legs
Pawing at the green porcelain doors of the remote Heavens.
Fly, mares!
Strain your utmost,
Scatter the milky dust of stars,
Or the tiger sun will leap upon you and destroy you
With one lick of his vermilion˙ tongue.   [= bright red]

AMY LOWELL

BALLAD OF SPRINGHILL
THE SPRINGHILL MINE DISASTER

In the town of Springhill, Nova Scotia,
Down in the dark of the Cumberland Mine,
There's blood on the coal and the miners lie
In the roads that never saw sun nor sky.

In the town of Springhill, you don't sleep easy,
Often the earth will tremble and roll,
When the earth is restless, miners die,
Bone and blood is the price of coal.

In the town of Springhill, Nova Scotia,
Late in the year of fifty-eight,
Day still comes and the sun still shines,
But it's dark as the grave in the Cumberland Mine.

Down at the coal face, miners working,
Rattle of the belt and the cutter's blade,
Rumble of rock and the walls close round
The living and the dead men two miles down.

Twelve men lay two miles from the pitshaft,
Twelve men lay in the dark and sang,
Long, hot days in the miner's tomb,
It was three feet high and a hundred long.

Three days passed and the lamps gave out,
And Caleb Rushton he up and said:
"There's no more water nor light nor bread
So we'll live on songs and hope instead."

Listen for the shouts of the bareface miners,
Listen through the rubble for a rescue team,
Six-hundred feet of coal and slag,
Hope imprisoned in a three-foot seam.

Eight days passed and some were rescued,
Leaving the dead to lie alone,
Through all their lives they dug a grave,
Two miles of earth for a marking stone.

EWAN MACCOLL & PEGGY SEEGER

THE LESSON

Chaos ruled OK in the classroom
as bravely the teacher walked in
the nooligans ignored him
his voice was lost in the din

"The theme for today is violence
and homework will be set
I'm going to teach you a lesson
one that you'll never forget"

He picked on a boy who was shouting
and throttled him then and there
then garotted the girl behind him
(the one with grotty hair)

Then sword in hand he hacked his way
between the chattering rows
"First come, first severed" he declared
"fingers, feet, or toes"

He threw the sword at a latecomer
it struck with deadly aim
then pulling out a shotgun
he continued with his game

The first blast cleared the backrow
(where those who skive hang out)
they collapsed like rubber dinghies
when the plug's pulled out

"Please may I leave the room sir?"
a trembling vandal enquired
"Of course you may" said the teacher
put the gun to his temple and fired

The Head popped a head round the doorway
to see why a din was being made
nodded understandingly
then tossed in a grenade

And when the ammo was well spent
with blood on every chair
Silence shuffled forward
with its hands up in the air

[= dead bodies] The teacher surveyed the carnage*
the dying and the dead
He waggled a finger severely
"Now let that be a lesson" he said

ROGER McGOUGH

"Jackets doffed they swing axes and chop away just above ground." (p. 87)

FIRST DAY AT SCHOOL

A millionbillionwillion miles from home
Waiting for the bell to go. (To go where?)
Why are they all so big, other children?
So noisy? So much at home they
must have been born in uniform.
Lived all their lives in playgrounds.
Spent the years inventing games
that don't let me in. Games
that are rough, that swallow you up.

And the railings.
All around, the railings.
Are they to keep out wolves and monsters?
Things that carry off and eat children?
Things you don't take sweets from?
Perhaps they're to stop us getting out.
Running away from the lessins. Lessin.
What does a lessin look like?
Sounds small and slimy.
They keep them in glassrooms.
Whole rooms made out of glass. Imagine.

I wish I could remember my name.
Mummy said it would come in useful.
Like wellies. When there's puddles.
Yellowwellies. I wish she was here.
I think my name is sewn on somewhere.
Perhaps the teachers will read it for me.
Tea-cher. The one who makes the tea.

ROGER McGOUGH

THE IDENTIFICATION

So you think its Stephen?
Then I'd best make sure
Be on the safe side as it were.
Ah, theres been a mistake. The hair
you see, its black, now Stephens fair . . .
What's that? The explosion?
Of course, burnt black. Silly of me.
I should have known. Then lets get on.

The face, is that a face I ask?
That mask of charred wood
blistered, scarred could
that have been a child's face?
The sweater, where intact, looks
in fact all too familiar.
But one must be sure.

The scoutbelt. Yes thats his.
I recognize the studs he hammered in
not a week ago. At the age
when boys get clothes-conscious
now you know. It's almost
certainly Stephen. But one must
be sure. Remove all trace of doubt.
Pull out every splinter of hope.

Pockets. Empty the pockets.
Handkerchief? Could be any schoolboy's.
Dirty enough. Cigarettes?
Oh this can't be Stephen.
I dont allow him to smoke you see.
He wouldn't disobey me. Not his father.

But thats his penknife. Thats his alright.
And thats his key on the keyring
Gran gave him just the other night.
So this must be him.

I think I know what happened
.   .   .   .   . about the cigarettes
No doubt he was minding them
for one of the older boys.
Yes thats it.
Thats him.
Thats our Stephen.

ROGER McGOUGH

A MUCKY JOB

*I're done some rum things in my time
I aren't one ta be beat
I'll tell ya now about one day
When I darned near lost ma feet.

See, ma brothers all went out one day
Left me and ma alone
Ta feed and tend ta all the pigs
While they wuz havin' fun.

You mix the grub I say ta mum
And I'll go in and feed 'em.
Alright she say, that suit me fine
Gal Maggie, let's get goin'.

* Written in the dialect of Norfolk, England.

So pails in hand and baited breath
I hopped into that sty
My word, them pigs all charged at me
Cort, I let out a cry.

Up went the pail, the meal was out
And afore I could turn around
Them beggars had me down an' all
Headfirst on the ground.

Mother say, what are you doin'
Face down in that dirt
Get up ya silly gal she say
Do you'll get really hurt.

Well up I got, a proper sight
All muck from head ta toe
Well don't just stand there gal she say
Go on, have another go.

'Cos now they'd got some grub ta eat
The next time in was easy
They din't pay na heed ta me
I hopped in and out right breezy.

But when I'd finished I'll tell you
My poor old back was achin'
So do you think a me you lot
When you next eat your bit a bacon!

MAWTHER MAGGIE

THE PASSIONATE SHEPHERD TO HIS LOVE

Come live with me, and be my love,
And we will all the pleasures prove,
That Vallies, groves, hills and fields,
Woods, or steepie mountain yields.

And we will sit upon the Rocks,
Seeing the Shepherds feed their flocks,
By shallow Rivers, to whose falls,
Melodious birds sing Madrigals˙.   [= kind of song]

And I will make thee beds of Roses,
And a thousand fragrant posies,
A cap of flowers, and a kirtle˙,   [= skirt]
Embroidered all with leaves of Mirtle.

A gown made of the finest wool,
Which from our pretty Lambs we pull,
Fair lined slippers for the cold:
With buckles of the purest gold.

A belt of straw, and Ivy buds,
With Coral clasps and Amber studs,
And if these pleasures may thee move,
Come live with me, and be my love.

The Shepherds Swains˙ shall dance and sing,   [= boy helpers]
For thy delight each May-morning,
If these delights thy mind may move;
Then live with me, and be my love.

CHRISTOPHER MARLOWE

133

MEAN SONG

Snickles and podes,
Ribble and grodes:
That's what I wish you.

A nox in the groot,
A root in the stoot
And a gock in the forbeshaw, too.

Keep out of sight
For fear that I might
Glom you a gravely snave.

Don't show your face
Around any place
Or you'll get one flack snack in the bave.

EVE MERRIAM

FRYING PAN IN THE MOVING VAN

A new family's coming to live next door to me.
I looked in the moving van to see what I could see.
What did you see?
Tell, tell, tell.

Well,
I saw a frying pan in the moving van.
What else did you see?
Tell, tell, tell.

Well,
I saw a rocking chair and a stuffed teddy bear
and a frying pan in the moving van.
What else did you see?
Tell, tell, tell.

Well,
I saw a rug for the floor and a boat with an oar
and a rocking chair and a stuffed teddy bear
and a frying pan in the moving van.
> *What else did you see?*
> *Tell, tell, tell.*

Well, I saw a leather boot and a basket of fruit
and a rug for the floor and a boat with an oar
and a rocking chair and a stuffed teddy bear
and a frying pan in the moving van.
> *What else did you see?*
> *Tell, tell, tell.*

Well, I saw a TV set and a Ping-Pong net
and a leather boot and a basket of fruit
and a rug for the floor and a boat with an oar
and a rocking chair and a stuffed teddy bear
and a frying pan in the moving van.
> *What else did you see?*
> *Tell, tell, tell.*

Well, I saw a steamer trunk and a double-decker bunk
and a TV set and a Ping-Pong net
and a leather boot and a basket of fruit
and a rug for the floor and a boat with an oar
and a rocking chair and a stuffed teddy bear
and a frying pan in the moving van.
What else did you see?
Tell, tell, tell.

Well, I saw a lamp with a shade and a jug of lemonade
and a steamer trunk and a double-decker bunk
and a TV set and a Ping-Pong net
and a leather boot and a basket of fruit
and a rug for the floor and a boat with an oar
and a rocking chair and a stuffed teddy bear
and a frying pan in the moving van.
What else did you see?
Tell, tell, tell.

Well, since you ask it:
I saw a wicker basket
and a violin and a rolling pin and a vegetable bin
and a lamp with a shade and a jug of lemonade
    and a garden spade
and a steamer trunk and a double-decker bunk
    and a Chinese model junk
and a TV set and a Ping-Pong net
    and a framed silhouette
and a leather boot and a basket of fruit
    and a baseball suit
and a rug for the floor and a boat with an oar
    and a knob for a door
and a rocking chair and a stuffed teddy bear
    and plastic dinnerware
and an electric fan and a bent tin can
    and a frying pan and
THAT'S ALL I SAW IN THE MOVING VAN.

EVE MERRIAM

TEEVEE

In the house
of Mr and Mrs Spouse
he and she
would watch teevee
and never a word
between them spoken
until the day
the set was broken.

Then "How do you do?"
said he to she,
"I don't believe
that we've met yet.
Spouse is my name.
What's yours?" he asked.

"Why, mine's the same!"
said she to he,
"Do you suppose that we could be —?"

But the set came suddenly right about,
and so they never did find out.

EVE MERRIAM

HEARING YOUR WORDS,
AND NOT A WORD AMONG THEM

Hearing your words, and not a word among them
Tuned to my liking, on a salty day
When inland woods were pushed by winds that flung them
Hissing to leeward like a ton of spray,
I thought how off Matinicus the tide
Came pounding in, came running through the Gut,
While from the Rock the warning whistle cried,
And children whimpered, and the doors blew shut;
There in the autumn when the men go forth,
With slapping skirts the island women stand
In gardens stripped and scattered, peering north,
With dahlia tubers dripping from the hand:
The wind of their endurance, driving south,
Flattened your words against your speaking mouth.

EDNA ST. VINCENT MILLAY

A LITTLE WORM

Today I saw a little worm
Wriggling on his belly.
Perhaps he'd like to come inside
And see what's on the Telly.

SPIKE MILLIGAN

THE DOG LOVERS

So they bought you
And kept you in a
Very good home
Central heating
TV

A deep freeze
A *very* good home –
No one to take you
For that lovely long run –
But otherwise
"A *very* good home."
They fed you Pal and Chum
But not that lovely long run,
Until, mad with energy and boredom
You ecaped – and ran and ran and ran
Under a car.
Today they will cry for you –
Tomorrow they will buy another dog.

SPIKE MILLIGAN

SONNET XVI*

When I consider how my light is spent,
   E're half my days, in this dark world and wide,
   And that one Talent which is death to hide,
   Lodg'd with me useless, though my Soul more bent

* On his blindness.

To serve therewith my Maker, and present
   My true account, least he returning chide,
   Doth God exact day-labour, light deny'd,
   I fondly ask; But patience to prevent
That murmur, soon replies, God doth not need
   Either man's work or his own gifts, who best
   Bear his mild yoak*, they serve him best, his State
Is Kingly. Thousands at his bidding speed
   And post o're Land and Ocean without rest:
   They also serve who only stand and wait.

[= yoke]

JOHN MILTON

PAUSE

I was just about to say to my daughter:
Look what beautiful eyes that horse has.
When I suddenly stopped and thought:
Maybe horses aren't supposed to have eyes like that.

ADRIAN MITCHELL

DUMB INSOLENCE

I'm big for ten years old
Maybe that's why they get at me

Teachers, parents, cops
Always getting at me

When they get at me

I don't hit em
They can do you for that

I don't swear at em
They can do you for that

I stick my hands in my pockets
And stare at them

And while I stare at them
I think about sick

They call it dumb insolence

They don't like it
But they can't do you for it

ADRIAN MITCHELL

NOT A VERY CHEERFUL SONG, I'M AFRAID

There was a gloomy lady,
With a gloomy duck and a gloomy drake,
And they all three wandered gloomily,
Beside a gloomy lake,
On a gloomy, gloomy, gloomy, gloomy, gloomy, gloomy day.

Now underneath that gloomy lake
The gloomy lady's gone.
But the gloomy duck and the gloomy drake
Swim on and on and on,
On a gloomy, gloomy, gloomy, gloomy, gloomy, gloomy day.

ADRIAN MITCHELL

BACK IN THE PLAYGROUND BLUES

Dreamed I was in a school playground, I was about four feet high
Yes dreamed I was back in the playground, and standing about four feet
high
The playground was three miles long and the playground was five miles
wide

It was broken black tarmac with a high fence all around
Broken black dusty tarmac with a high fence running all around
And it had a special name to it, they called it The Killing Ground.

Got a mother and a father, they're a thousand miles away
The Rulers of the Killing Ground are coming out to play
Everyone thinking: who they going to play with today?

    You get it for being Jewish
    Get it for being black
    Get it for being chicken
    Get it for fighting back
    You get it for being big and fat
    Get it for being small
    O those who get it get it and get it
    For any damn thing at all

Sometimes they take a beetle, tear off its six legs one by one
Beetle on its black back rocking in the lunchtime sun
But a beetle can't beg for mercy, a beetle's not half the fun

Heard a deep voice talking, it had that iceberg sound;
"It prepares them for Life" – but I have never found
Any place in my life that's worse than The Killing Ground.

ADRIAN MITCHELL

OVERHEARD ON A SALTMARSH

Nymph, nymph, what are your beads?

Green glass, goblin. Why do you stare at them?

Give them me.

No.

Give them me. Give them me.

No.

Then I will howl all night in the reeds.
Lie in the mud and howl for them.

Goblin, why do you love them so?

They are better than stars or water,
Better than voices of winds that sing,
Better than any man's fair daughter,
Your green glass beads on a silver ring.

Hush, I stole them out of the moon.

Give me your beads, I desire them.

No.

I will howl in a deep lagoon
For your green glass beads, I love them so.
Give them me. Give them.

No.

HAROLD MONRO

143

THE COMPUTER'S FIRST CHRISTMAS CARD

jollymerry
hollyberry
jollyberry
merryholly
happyjolly
jollyjelly
jellybelly
bellymerry
hollyheppy
jollyMolly
marryJerry
merryHarry
happyBarry
heppyJarry
boppyheppy
berryjorry
jorryjolly
moppyjelly
Mollymerry
Jerryjolly
bellyboppy
jorryhoppy
hollymoppy
Barrymerry
Jarryhappy
happyboppy
boppyjolly
jollymerry
merrymerry
merrymerry
merryChris
ammerryasa
Chrismerry
asMERRYCHR
YSANTHEMUM

EDWIN MORGAN

"Then I shall tie it very tight . . . and hang head downward from the ceiling." (p. 94)

INTERFERENCE

bringing you live
the final preparations
for this great mission
should be coasting
the rings of Saturn
two years time
cloudless sky, and
an unparalleled
world coverage
we have countdown
          ten
may not have told you
          nine
the captain's mascot
          eight
miniaturized gonk
          seven
chief navigator
          six
had twins Tuesday
          five
the Eiffel Tower for
          four
comparison, gantries
          three
aside, so the fuel
          two
huge cloud of
          one
a perfect
          a half
I don't quite
          a quarter
something has clearly
          an eighth
we do not have lift-off

a sixteenth
we do not have lift-off
a thirty-second
we do not have lift-off
a sixty-fourth
we do not have lift-off
a hundred and twenty-eighth
wo de nat hove loft-iff

EDWIN MORGAN

THE FIRST MEN ON MERCURY

– We come in peace from the third planet.
Would you take us to your leader?

– Bawr stretter! Bawr. Bawr. Stretterhawl?

– This is a little plastic model
of the solar system, with working parts.
You are here and we are there and we
are now here with you, is this clear?

– Gawl horrop. Bawr. Abawrhannahanna!

– Where we come from is blue and white
with brown, you see we call the brown
here 'land', the blue is 'sea', and the white
is 'clouds' over land and sea, we live
on the surface of the brown land,
all round is sea and clouds. We are 'men'.
Men come –

– Glawp men! Gawrbenner menko. Menhawl?

– Men come in peace from the third planet
which we call 'earth'. We are earthmen.
Take us earthmen to your leader.

–Thmen? Thmen? Bawr. Bawrhossop.
Yuleeda tan hanna. Harrabost yuleeda.

146

– I am the yuleeda. You see my hands,
we carry no benner, we come in peace.
The spaceways are all stretterhawn.

– Glawn peacemen all horrobhanna tantko!
Tan come at'mstrossop. Glawp yuleeda!

– Atoms are peacegawl in our harraban.
Menbat worrabost from tan hannahanna.

– ou men we know bawrhossoptant. Bawr.
We know yuleeda. Go strawg backspetter quick.

– We cantantabawr, tantingko backspetter now!

– Banghapper now! Yes, third planet back.
Yuleeda will go back blue, white, brown
nowhanna! There is no more talk.

– Gawl han fasthapper?

– No. You must go back to your planet.
Go back in peace, take what you have gained
but quickly.

– Stretterworra gawl, gawl . . .

– Of course, but nothing is ever the same,
now is it? You'll remember Mercury.

EDWIN MORGAN

IN THE CASE OF LOBSTERS

There are
2 methods some put
the live lobster
in boiling
water for the best
taste
but
with a microphone
you can hear screams
of pain if
in the case of lobsters
one can speak of such a thing
as pain

Others
for humanitarian reasons
put it in cold
then bring to the boil

PETRA VON MORSTEIN
(translated by Rosemarie Waldrop)

THE PIG

The pig, if I am not mistaken,
Supplies us sausage, ham, and bacon.
Let others say his heart is big –
I call it stupid of the pig.

OGDEN NASH

GRANNY GRANNY PLEASE COMB MY HAIR

Granny Granny
please comb my hair
you always take your time
you always take such care

You put me to sit on a cushion
between your knees
you rub a little coconut oil
parting gentle as a breeze

Mummy Mummy
she's always in a hurry – hurry
rush
she pulls my hair
sometimes she tugs

But Granny
you have all the time in the world
and when you're finished
you always turn my head and say
"Now who's a nice girl."

GRACE NICHOLS

SEA TIMELESS SONG

Hurricane come
and hurricane go
but sea . . . sea timeless
sea timeless
sea timeless
sea timeless
sea timeless

Hibiscus bloom
then dry-wither so
but sea . . . sea timeless
sea timeless
sea timeless
sea timeless
sea timeless

Tourist come
and tourist go
but sea . . . sea timeless
sea timeless
sea timeless
sea timeless
sea timeless

GRACE NICHOLS

150

ROAD UP

What's wrong with the road?
Why all this hush? –
They've given an anaesthetic
In the lunch-hour rush.

They've shaved off the tarmac
With a pneumatic drill,
And bandaged the traffic
To a dead standstill.

Surgeons in shirt-sleeves
Bend over the patient,
Intent on a major
Operation.

Don't dare sneeze!
Don't dare shout!
The road is having
Its appendix out.

NORMAN NICHOLSON

BOY FLYING

Flying,
   He saw the earth flat as a plate,
   As if there were no hills, as if houses
   Were only roofs, as if the trees
   Were only the leaves that covered
   The treetops. He could see the shadows
   The clouds cast when they sailed over the fields,
   He could see the river like the silver track
   Left by a snail, and roads narrow as ribbons.

   He could not see Mickey French next door,
   In bed with a cold, nor his two sisters
   Playing "Happy Families" as they watched
   The television. He could not see his kitten.

Flying,
   He felt the air as solid as water
   When he spread his fingers against it.
   He felt it cool against his face, he felt
   His hair whipped. He felt weightless
   As if he were hollow, he felt the sun
   Enormously bright and warm on his back,
   He felt his eyes watering. He felt
   The small, moist drops the clouds held.

   He could not feel the grass, he could not
   Feel the rough stones of the garden wall.
   He could not remember the harsh, dry bark
   Of the apple tree against his knees.

Flying,
   He could hear the wind hissing, the note
   Changed when he turned his head. He heard
   His own voice when he sang. Very faintly,
   He heard the school bus as it grumbled
   Past the church, he thought he could hear
   The voices of the people as they shouted
   In amazement when they saw him swoop and glide.

He could not hear the birds sing, nor the chalk
Squeak against the blackboard, nor the mower
As it whirred along, nor the clock tick.
He could not hear the bacon sizzle in the pan,
He could not hear his friend calling him.

LESLIE NORRIS

"I wonder how much air
there is in this balloon,"
said my brother.
"Well bust it and see," I said.
"But then the air will escape,"
he said: him being a year
and one month older than me.
"No it won't," I said.
"It will still be in the room
and you can always get it back
again by blowing up another
balloon."
"No! That's rot," he said.
"If I bust this balloon
I shall never know how much air
was in it."
"Yes you will."
"No I won't."
"Yes you will."
"No I won't."
I burst his balloon,
He cried aloud,
"Now look what you've done.
You've stolen my air."
"You can always get it back,"
I said.
"No I can't," he moaned
"I've no more balloons."

O. O'NEILL

UNDER THE STAIRS

Look in the dark alcove under the stairs:
a paintbrush steeped in turpentine, its hairs

softening for use; rat-poison in a jar;
bent spoons for prising lids; a spare fire-bar;

the shaft of a broom; a tyre; assorted nails;
a store of candles for when the light fails.

FRANK ORMSBY

THE WAR SONG OF DINAS VAWR

The mountain sheep are sweeter,
But the valley sheep are fatter;
We therefore deemed it meeter
To carry off the latter.
We made an expedition;
We met a host and quelled it;
We forced a strong position,
And killed the men who held it.

On Dyfed's richest valley,
Where herds of kine were browsing,
We made a mighty sally,
To furnish our carousing.
Fierce warriors rushed to meet us;
We met them and o'erthrew them:
They struggled hard to beat us;
But we conquered them and slew them.

As we drove our prize at leisure,
The king marched forth to catch us;
His rage surpassed all measure,
But his people could not match us.
He fled to his hall pillars;

And, ere our force we led off,
Some sacked his house and cellars,
While others cut his head off.

We there, in strife bewildering,
Spilt blood enough to swim in:
We orphaned many children,
And widowed many women.
The eagles and the ravens
We glutted with our foemen:
The heroes and the cravens,
The spearmen and the bowmen.

We brought away from battle,
And much their land bemoaned them,
Two thousand head of cattle,
And the head of him who owned them:
Edynfed, King of Dyfed,
His head was borne before us;
His wine and beasts supplied our feasts,
And his overthrow, our chorus.

THOMAS LOVE PEACOCK

ELDORADO*

[= dressed]

Gaily bedight*,
A gallant knight
In sunshine and in shadow,
Had journeyed long,
Singing a song,
In search of Eldorado.

But he grew old –
This knight so bold –
And o'er his heart a shadow
Fell, as he found
No spot of ground
That looked like Eldorado.

And as his strength
Failed him at length,
He met a pilgrim shadow:
"Shadow," said he,
"Where can it be,
This land of Eldorado?"

"Over the mountains
Of the Moon,
Down the valley of Shadow,
Ride, boldly ride,"
The shade replied,
"If you seek for Eldorado."

EDGAR ALLEN POE

* An imagined place in South America that Spanish
explorers believed was full of gold.

*A DREAM WITHIN A DREAM

I stand amid the roar
Of a surf-tormented shore,
And I hold within my hand
Grains of the golden sand –
How few! yet how they creep
Through my fingers to the deep,
While I weep – while I weep!
Oh God! can I not grasp
Them with a tighter clasp?
O God! can I not save
One from the pitiless wave?
Is *all* that we see or seem
But a dream within a dream?

EDGAR ALLAN POE

*Verse 2 only.

THE ECLIPSE

Louis the Fourteenth also called the Sun King
often sat on a chamberpot-chair
toward the end of his reign
one night when it was very dark
the Sun King rose from his bed
went to sit on his chamberpot-chair
and disappeared.

JACQUES PRÉVERT
(translated by Laurence Ferlinghetti)

157

FIGHTING BACK

We all used to pick on him,
He used to stand there and let us.
We called him scabs.
He was ugly beyond words.
I hated him.
He used to slaver and spit when he spoke.
We used to call him names, bad names,
    horrible names.
Some teachers hated him.
They said he was disgusting.
Some said it was disgusting the way we
    picked on him.
But one day he fought back.
I stood there amazed.
He had hit me.
I was stunned!
Then I hit him back.
He got me in the eye.
Everyone stood quiet as though in a
    trance.
"He fights back!" I shouted.
"The dog fights back!"

GEOFFREY PROUDLOCK

BIG FEARS

Twenty-five feet above Sian's house
hangs a thick wire cable
that droops and sags between two
electricity pylons.
A notice says it carries 40,000 volts
from one metallic scarecrow to the next,

then on to the next and the next
right across the countryside to the city.
The cable sways above Sian's council house
making her radio crackle and sometimes
making her television go on the blink.

If it's a very windy night
Sian gets frightened because she
thinks the cable might snap,
fall onto the roof and electrocute
everyone as they sleep.

This is Sian's Big Fear.

Outside Matthew's bedroom there
is a tall tree. Taller than the house.
In summer it is heavy with huge leaves.
In winter it stands lonely as a morning moon.

On a windy night, Matthew worries
that the tree might be blown down
and crash through his bedroom window.
It would certainly kill him and his cat
if it wasn't in its own cardboard box.

This is Matthew's Big Fear.

Outside Karen's bedroom there's nothing
but a pleasant view, meadows, hedges, sheep
and some distant gentle hills.
There's nothing sinister, nothing to worry about.

But in the dark Karen thinks
the darting shapes on the ceiling
are really the shadows of a ghost's
great cold hands and that the night noises
made by the water pipes are the
screeches and groans of attic skeletons.

JOHN RICE

THE HONEY POT

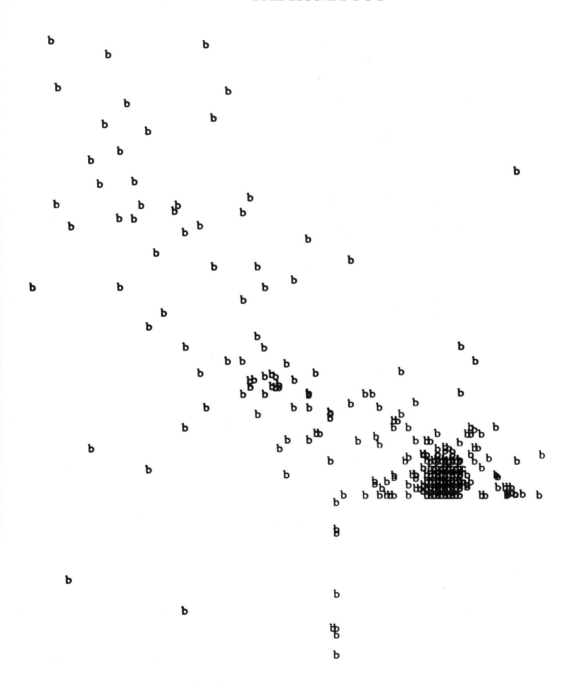

ALAN RIDDELL

"And then I'd be a foxy fox . . . I'm a master of disguise, you see." (p. 99)

```
UR 2  GOOD
   2  ME
   2  BE
   4  GOT
  ──
  10
```

PLAYING WITH WORDS

You can play with dice
You can play with cards
You can play with a ball
You can play with words

words
words
words
words
words
words
banana
words
words
words
words
words

MICHAEL ROSEN

words

DOPEY AND DOZEY

Dopey's wife sent him down town
to fetch a bucket of ice.
He came back with a pail of water
"I got this half price
because it was melted."

Dopey and Dozey were in jail.
They were trying to find a way out
"I know," says Dopey
"I'll shine my torch up to that window
you crawl up the beam of light
and open up that window."
Dozey didn't like the sound of that.
"I know you, Dopey,
I'd get halfway up the beam
and you'd turn the light off."

(Adapted from a variety of sources by MICHAEL ROSEN)

TOOTHPASTE

Who's been at the toothpaste?
I know some of you do it right
and you squeeze the tube from the bottom
and you roll up the tube as it gets used up, don't you?

But somebody
somebody here –
you know who you are
you dig your thumb in
anywhere, anyhow
and you've turned that tube of toothpaste
into a squashed sock.
You've made it so hard to use
it's like trying to get toothpaste
out of a packet of nuts.

You know who you are.
I won't ask you to come out here now
but you know who you are.

And then you went and left the top off didn't you?
So the toothpaste turned to cement.

People who do things like that should . . .
you should be ashamed of yourself.

I am.

MICHAEL ROSEN

HOT FOOD

We sit down to eat
and the potato's a bit hot
so I only put a little bit on my fork
and I blow
whooph whooph
until it's cool
just cool
then into the mouth
nice.
And there's my brother
he's doing the same
whooph whooph
into the mouth
nice.
There's my mum
she's doing the same
whooph whooph

into the mouth
nice.

But my dad.
My dad.
What does he do?
He stuffs a great big chunk of potato
into his mouth.
then
that really does it.
His eyes pop out
he flaps his hands
he blows, he puffs, he yells
he bobs his head up and down
he spits bits of potato
all over his plate
and he turns to us and he says,
"Watch out everybody –
the potato's very hot."

MICHAEL ROSEN

HUMPTY DUMPTY
(written using only names from the telephone directory)

Humm Tee Dim Tay
Sato Nawol
Huntly Dumke
Hudd Agate Fall
Alder King Soss
Isan Dorley Kinsman
Coode Dant Pot
Humphrey Duhig Adda Arr Gaine

MICHAEL ROSEN
SUSANNA STEELE

TRANSFORMATIONS

My little son enters
the room and says
"you are a vulture
I am a mouse"

I put away my book
wings and claws
grow out of me

their ominous shadows
race on the walls
I am a vulture
he is a mouse

"you are a wolf
I am a goat"
I walked around the table
and am a wolf
windowpanes gleam
like fangs
in the dark

165

while he runs to his mother
safe
his head hidden in the warmth of her dress

TADEUSZ RÓŻEWICZ
(translated by Czeslaw Milosz)

THE CLOCK ON THE WALL

My city collapsed
The clock was still on the wall
Our neighbourhood collapsed
The clock was still on the wall
The street collapsed
The clock was still on the wall
The square collapsed
The clock was still on the wall
The house collapsed
The clock was still on the wall
The wall collapsed
The clock
Ticked on

SAMIH AL-QASIM

MANUAL SYSTEM

Mary has a thingamajig clamped on her ears
And sits all day taking plugs out and sticking plugs in.
Flashes and flashes – voices and voices
   calling for ears to pour words in;
Faces at the ends of wires asking for other faces
   at the ends of other wires:
All day taking plugs out and sticking plugs in,
Mary has a thingamajig clamped on her ears.

CARL SANDBURG

ELEPHANTS ARE DIFFERENT TO DIFFERENT PEOPLE

Wilson and Pilcer and Snack stood before the zoo elephant.

Wilson said, "What is its name? Is it from Asia or Africa?
Who feeds it? Is it a he or a she? How old is it? Do they have
twins? How much does it cost to feed? How much does it weigh?
If it dies how much will another one cost? If it dies what will
they use the bones, the fat, and the hide for? What use is it
besides to look at?"

Pilcer didn't have any questions: he was murmuring to himself,
"It's a house by itself, walls and windows, the ears come from
tall cornfields, by God; the architect of those legs was a
workman, by God; he stands like a bridge out across deep
water; the face is sad and the eyes are kind; I know elephants
are good to babies."

Snack looked up and down and at last said to himself, "He's a
tough son-of-a-gun outside and I'll bet he's got a strong heart, I'll
bet he's strong as a copper-riveted boiler inside."

They didn't put up any arguments.
They didn't throw anything in each other's faces.
Three men saw the elephant three ways
And let it go at that.
They didn't spoil a sunny Sunday afternoon;
"Sunday comes only once a week," they told each other.

CARL SANDBURG

167

GARGOYLE

I saw a mouth jeering. A smile of melted red iron ran over it. Its laugh
    was full of nails rattling. It was a child's dream of a mouth.
A fist hit the mouth: knuckles of gun-metal driven by an electric wrist
    and shoulder. It was a child's dream of an arm.
The fist hit the mouth over and over, again and again. The mouth bled
    melted iron, and laughed its laughter of nails rattling.
And I saw the more the fist pounded the more the mouth laughed. The
    fist is pounding and pounding, and the mouth answering.

CARL SANDBURG

WARS

In the old wars drum of hoofs and the beat of shod feet.
In the new wars hum of motors and the tread of rubber tires.
In the wars to come silent wheels and whirr of rods not yet dreamed out
    in the heads of men.

In the old wars clutches of short swords and jabs into faces with spears.
In the new wars long-range guns and smashed walls, guns running a spit
    of metal and men falling in tens and twenties.
In the wars to come new silent deaths, new silent hurlers not yet
    dreamed out in the heads of men.

In the old wars kings quarreling and thousands of men following.
In the new wars kings quarreling and millions of men following.
In the wars to come kings kicked under the dust and millions of men
    following great causes not yet dreamed out in the heads of men.

CARL SANDBURG

from THE PEOPLE, YES

"The man put green spectacles on his cow and fed her sawdust.
Maybe she would believe it was grass.
But she didn't. She died on him."

"Get off this estate."
"What for?"
"Because it's mine."
"Where did you get it?"
"From my father."
"Where did he get it?"
"From his father."
"And where did he get it?"
"He fought for it."
"Well, I'll fight you for it."

Why did the children
put beans in their ears
when the one thing we told the children
they must not do
was put beans in their ears?

Why did the children pour molasses on the cat
when the one thing we told the children
they must not do
was pour molasses on the cat?

A high pressure salesman jumped off the Brooklyn Bridge and was saved
by a policeman. But it didn't take him long to sell the idea to the
policeman. So together they jumped off the bridge.

"The number 42 will win this raffle, that's my number." And when he
won they asked him whether he guessed the number or had a
system. He said he had a system, "I took up the old family album
and there on page 7 was my grandfather and grandmother both on
page 7. I said to myself this is easy for 7 times 7 is the number that
will win and 7 times 7 is 42."

[outside kitchen used in warm weather] An Ohio man bundled up a tin roof of a summer kitchen* and
sent it to a motor car maker with a complaint of his car
not giving service. In three weeks a new car arrived for him
and a letter: "We regret delay in shipment but your car
was received in a very bad order."

"Isn't that an iceberg on the horizon, Captain?"
"Yes, Madam."
"What if we get in a collision with it?"
"The iceberg, Madam, will move right along
    as though nothing had happened."

"You will see me surrender,"
said one old Viking,
"When hair grows in the palm of my hand."

"What are you fellows scared of? nothing?"
this too they asked the old Viking who said,
"Yes, one thing we are scared of, we are scared
the sky might come tumbling down on us."

"There on the same track I saw the westbound passenger train coming
    fifty miles an hour and the eastbound freight forty miles an hour."
"And what did you think?"
"I thought what a hell of a way to run a railroad!"

"I am John Jones."
"Take a chair."

"Yes, and I am the son of John
Throckmorton Jones."
"Is that possible? Take two chairs."

"What's the matter up there?"
"Playing soldier."
"But soldiers don't make that kind of noise."
"We're playing the kind of soldier that
makes that kind of noise."

Phone girl: "I'm sorry I gave you the wrong number."
Man: "I'm sorry too, I know it was a perfectly good
number you gave me but I just couldn't use it."

Listen to the laboratory man tell what you are
    made of, man, listen while he takes you apart.
Weighing 150 pounds you hold 3,500 cubic feet of
    gas – oxygen, hydrogen, nitrogen.
From the 22 pounds and 10 ounces of carbon in
    you is the filling for 9,000 lead pencils.
In your blood are 50 grains of iron and in the rest
    of your frame enough iron to make a spike
    that would hold your weight.
From your 50 ounces of phosphorus could be made
    800,000 matches and elsewhere in your physical
    premises are hidden 60 lumps of sugar, 20 tea-
    spoons of salt, 38 quarts of water, two ounces

of lime, and scatterings of starch, chloride of
potash, magnesium, sulphur, hydrochloric acid.

Lawyer: What was the distance between
          the two towns?
Witness: Two miles as the cry flows.
Lawyer: You mean as the crow flies.
Judge: No, he means as the fly crows.

Who was the St. Louis mathematician who figured it cost an average of
          £37,000 to kill each soldier killed in the World War?
He figured too on a way of offering, in case of war, £1,000, one grand,
          to every deserting soldier.
Each army, the idea ran, would buy off the other before the war could
          get started.

The Great Sphinx and the Pyramids say:
"Man passed this way and saw
a lot of ignorant besotted pharaohs."
The pink pagodas, jade rams and marble elephants
          of China say:
"Man came along here too ·
and met suave and cruel mandarins."
The temples and forums of Greece and Rome say:
"Man owned man here where man bought and sold
          man in the open slave auctions; by these chattels
          stone was piled on stone to make these now
          crumbled pavilions."
The medieval Gothic cathedrals allege:
"Mankind said prayers here for itself and for stiff-
          necked drunken robber barons."

And the skyscrapers of Manhattan, Detroit, Chi-
          cago, London, Paris, Berlin – what will they
          say when the hoarse and roaring years of
          their origin have sunk to a soft whispering?

CARL SANDBURG

MOTHER AND DAUGHTER

. . . my mother used to say that
in her youth it was thought to be
very fine to bind up your hair

with a dark purple headband – yes,
extremely fine indeed, although
for a girl whose hair is golden

like a torch flame better to wreathe
in it garlands of fresh flowers;
recently I saw a headband,

brightly coloured, from Sardis . . .

but for you, Cleis*, I do not have   [= Sappho's daughter]
a brightly coloured headband nor
do I know where I may find one . . .

SAPPHO
(translated by Josephine Balmer)

A CASE OF MURDER

They should not have left him there alone,
Alone that is except for the cat.
He was only nine, not old enough
To be left alone in a basement flat,
Alone, that is, except for the cat.
A dog would have been a different thing,
A big gruff dog with slashing jaws,
But a cat with round eyes mad as gold,
Plump as a cushion with tucked-in paws –
Better have left him with a fair-sized rat!
But what they did was leave him with a cat.
He hated that cat; he watched it sit,

A buzzing machine of soft black stuff,
He sat and watched and he hated it,
Snug in its fur, hot blood in a muff,
And its mad gold stare and the way it sat
Crooning dark warmth: he loathed all that.
So he took Daddy's stick and he hit the cat.
Then quick as a sudden crack in a glass
It hissed, black flash, to a hiding place
In the dust and dark beneath the couch,
And he followed the grin on his new-made face,
A wide-eyed, frightened snarl of a grin,
And he took the stick and he thrust it in,
Hard and quick in the furry dark,
The black fur squealed and he felt his skin
Prickle with sparks of dry delight.
Then the cat again came into sight,
Shot for the door that wasn't quite shut,
But the boy, quick too, slammed fast the door:
The cat, half-through, was cracked like a nut
And the soft black thud was dumped on the floor.
Then the boy was suddenly terrified
And he bit his knuckles and cried and cried;
But he had to do something with the dead
        thing there.
His eyes squeezed beads of salty prayer
But the wound of fear gaped wide and raw;
He dared not touch the thing with his hands
So he fetched a spade and shovelled it
And dumped the load of heavy fur
In the spidery cupboard under the stair
Where it's been for years, and though it died
It's grown in that cupboard and its hot low purr
Grows slowly louder year by year:
There'll not be a corner for the boy to hide
When the cupboard swells and all sides split
And the huge black cat pads out of it.

VERNON SCANNELL

WEATHER

It washes the floors off.
Then when it gets dry

You can sit in the park when the benches get dry
And you can walk on the street when it stops.

It's like a person who goes to do everything –
That's how the sky is.
The sky gets busy, she's working,
She's raining.
Then, when it stops raining, she doesn't do anything.
The sky is the sky,
And the sun comes out again.

YETTA SCHMIER

TAKING MEDICINE

In the bedroom I hide,
Mother calls,
My sister reads,
And I am silent,
I go to her very gravely going as silently and slowly as I can,
Suddenly I rush into the kitchen,

175

I say, quick, to get it over and done with,
With hot eyes I see mother pouring it out,
I bite the spoon the last drop,
Here I go,
When I have finished I run up the hall shouting,
"I have had my medicine go and have yours."

VALERIE SEEKINGS

GET UP AND SHUT THE DOOR

It happened one December night,
    And a dark night it was then,
That an old wife had puddings to make:
    She boiled them in the pan.

The wind blew cold from south and north.
    It blew across the floor:
The old man said to his old wife,
    "Get up and shut the door."

"My hands are in the pudding basin.
    Husband, can't you see?
If it has to wait a hundred years,
    It won't be shut by me."

"Their heads are green, and their hands are blue, and they went to sea in a sieve." (p. 114)

They made a pact between the two.
   They made it firm and sure:
"The one who is the first to speak
   Gets up and shuts the door."

Two gentlemen came passing by
   At twelve o'clock that night.
They couldn't see the house at all.
   Nor coal, nor candle-light.

They hit the house. "May we come in?
   Is anyone there?" they cried.
And then they went in through the door,
   For no one had replied.

First they ate the white puddings,
   Then they ate the black;
But never a word the old wife spoke,
   Though she was hopping mad.

Then one man said to the other man,
   "Here now! Take my knife.
You cut off the old man's beard,
   And I will kiss his wife."

"But there's no water in the house,
   So what shall we do then?"
"You'll have to use the pudding water
   Boiling in the pan."

Then up sprang the old man,
   An angry man was he:
"What! Kiss my wife before my face
   And slop that muck on me?"

Then up sprang the old wife
   And gave three skips on the floor:
"Husband, you were the first to speak:
   Get up and shut the door."

IAN SERRAILLIER

THE DIVER

I put on my aqua-lung and plunge,
Exploring, like a ship with a glass keel,
The secrets of the deep. Along my lazy road
On and on I steal –
Over waving bushes which at a touch explode
Into shrimps, then closing, rock to the tune of the tide;
Over crabs that vanish in puffs of sand.
Look, a string of pearls bubbling at my side
Breaks in my hand –
Those pearls were my breath! . . . Does that hollow hide
Some old Armada wreck in seaweed furled,
Crusted with barnacles, her cannon rusted,
The great *San Philip*? What bullion in her hold?
Pieces of eight, silver crowns, and bars of solid gold?

I shall never know. Too soon the clasping cold
Fastens on flesh and limb
And pulls me to the surface. Shivering, back I swim
To the beach, the noisy crowds, the ordinary world.

IAN SERRAILLIER

THE VISITOR

A crumbling churchyard, the sea and the moon;
The waves had gouged out grave and bone;
A man was walking, late and alone . . .

He saw a skeleton on the ground;
A ring on a bony finger he found.

He ran home to his wife and gave her the ring.
"Oh, where did you get it?" He said not a thing.

"It's the loveliest ring in the world," she said,
As it glowed on her finger. They slipped off to bed.

At midnight they woke. In the dark outside,
"Give me my ring!" a chill voice cried.

"What was that, William? What did it say?"
"Don't worry, my dear. It'll soon go away."

"I'm coming!" A skeleton opened the door.
"Give me my ring!" It was crossing the floor.

"What was that, William? What did it say?"
"Don't worry, my dear. It'll soon go away."

"I'm reaching you now! I'm climbing the bed."
The wife pulled the sheet right over her head.

It was torn from her grasp and tossed in the air:
"I'll drag you out of bed by the hair!"

"What was that, William? What did it say?"
"Throw the ring through the window! THROW IT AWAY!"

She threw it. The skeleton leapt from the sill,
Scooped up the ring and clattered downhill,
Fainter . . . and fainter . . . Then all was still.

IAN SERRAILLIER

MY FRIENDS

The man above was a murderer, the man below was a thief;
And I lay there in the bunk between, ailing beyond belief;
A weary armful of skin and bone, wasted with pain and grief.

My feet were froze, and the lifeless toes were purple and green
    and gray;
The little flesh that clung to my bones, you could punch it in
    holes like clay;
The skin on my gums was a sullen black, and slowly peeling
    away.

I was sure enough in a direful fix, and often I wondered why
They did not take the chance that was left and leave me alone
    to die,
Or finish me off with a dose of dope – so utterly lost was I.

But no; they brewed me the green-spruce tea, and nursed me
    there like a child;
And the homicide he was good to me, and bathed my sores
    and smiled;
And the thief he starved that I might be fed, and his eyes were
    kind and mild.

Yet they were woefully wicked men, and often at night in
    pain
I heard the murderer speak of his deed and dream it over
    again;
I heard the poor thief sorrowing for the dead self he had slain.

I'll never forget that bitter dawn, so evil, askew and gray,
When they wrapped me round in the skins of beasts and they
bore me to a sleigh,
And we started out with the nearest post an hundred miles
away.

I'll never forget the trail they broke, with its tense, un-
utterable woe;
And the crunch, crunch, crunch, as their snow-shoes sank
through the crust of the hollow snow;
And my breath would fail, and every beat of my heart was like
a blow.

And oftentimes I would die the death, yet wake up to life
anew;
The sun would be all ablaze on the waste, and the sky a
blighting blue.
And the tears would rise in my snow-blind eyes and furrow my
cheeks like dew.

And the camps we made when their strength outplayed and
the day was pinched and wan;
And oh, the joy of that blessed halt, and how I did dread the
dawn;
And how I hated the weary men who rose and dragged me on.

And oh, how I begged to rest, to rest – the snow was so sweet
a shroud;
And oh, how I cried when they urged me on, cried and cursed
them aloud;
Yet on they strained, all racked and pained, and sorely their
backs were bowed.

And then it was like a lurid dream, and I prayed for a swift
release.
From the ruthless ones who would not leave me to die alone
in peace;
Till I wakened up and I found myself at the post of the
Mounted Police.

And there was my friend the murderer, and there was my
    friend the thief,
With bracelets of steel around their wrists, and wicked
    beyond belief:
But when they come to God's judgement seat – may I be
    allowed the brief.

ROBERT SERVICE

THE DUKE OF CLARENCE'S DREAM

. . . As we paced along
Upon the giddy footing of the hatches,
Methought that Gloucester stumbled; and, in falling,
Struck me, that thought to stay him, overboard,
Into the tumbling billows of the main.
Lord, Lord! methought what pain it was to drown:
What dreadful noise of water in mine ears!
What sights of ugly death within mine eyes!

Methought I saw a thousand fearful wracks*;   [= shipwrecks]
A thousand men that fishes gnawed upon;
Wedges of gold, great anchors, heaps of pearl,
Inestimable stones, unvalued jewels,
All scattered in the bottom of the sea.
Some lay in dead men's skulls; and in those holes
Where eyes did once inhabit, there were crept,
As 'twere in scorn of eyes, reflecting gems,
That wooed the slimy bottom of the deep,
And mocked the dead bones that lay scattered by.

WILLIAM SHAKESPEARE
(from *Richard III*)

OZYMANDIAS

I met a traveller from an antique land
Who said: Two vast and trunkless legs of stone
Stand in the desert. Near them, on the sand,
Half sunk, a shatter'd visage lies, whose frown,
And wrinkled lip, and sneer of cold command,
Tell that its sculptor well those passions read
Which yet survive, stamp'd on these lifeless things,
The hand that mock'd them and the heart that fed:
And on the pedestal these words appear:
"My name is Ozymandias, king of kings:
Look on my works, ye Mighty, and despair!"
Nothing beside remains. Round the decay
Of that colossal wreck, boundless and bare
The lone and level sands stretch far away.

PERCY BYSSHE SHELLEY

EVENING: PONTE AL MARE, PISA

The sun is set; the swallows are asleep;
   The bats are flitting fast in the grey air;
The slow soft toads out of damp corners creep,
   And evening's breath, wandering here and there
Over the quivering surface of the stream,
Wakes not one ripple from its summer dream.

There is no dew on the dry grass to-night,
   Nor damp within the shadow of the trees;
The wind is intermitting, dry, and light;
   And in the inconstant motion of the breeze
The dust and straws are driven up and down,
And whirled about the pavement of the town.

Within the surface of the fleeting river
   The wrinkled image of the city lay,
Immovably unquiet, and for ever
   It trembles, but it never fades away . . .

PERCY BYSSHE SHELLEY

184

SILENT, BUT . . .

I may be silent, but
I'm thinking.
I may not talk, but
Don't mistake me for a wall.

TSUBOI SHIGEJI
(translated by Geoffrey Bownas and Anthony Thwaite)

HUNGRY MUNGRY

Hungry Mungry sat at supper,
Took his knife and spoon and fork,
Ate a bowl of mushroom soup, ate a slice of roasted pork,
Ate a dozen stewed tomatoes, twenty-seven deviled eggs,
Fifteen shrimps, nine baked potatoes,
Thirty-two fried chicken legs,
A shank of lamb, a boiled ham,
Two bowls of grits, some black-eye peas,
Four chocolate shakes, eight angel cakes,
Nine custard pies with Muenster cheese,
Ten pots of tea, and after he
Had eaten all that he was able,
He poured some broth on the tablecloth
And ate the kitchen table.

His parents said, "Oh Hungry Mungry, stop these silly jokes."
Mungry opened up his mouth, and "Gulp," he ate his folks.
And then he went and ate his house, all the bricks and wood,
And then he ate up all the people in the neighborhood.
Up came twenty angry policemen shouting, "Stop and cease."
Mungry opened up his mouth and "Gulp," he ate the police.
Soldiers came with tanks and guns.
Said Mungry, "They can't harm me."
He just smiled and licked his lips and ate the U.S. Army.

The President sent all his bombers – Mungry still was calm,
Put his head back, gulped the planes, and gobbled up the bomb.

He ate his town and ate the city – ate and ate and ate –
And then he said, "I think I'll eat the whole United States."

And so he ate Chicago first and munched the Water Tower,
And then he chewed on Pittsburgh but he found it rather sour.
He ate New York and Tennessee, and all of Boston town,

Then he drank the Mississippi River just to wash it down.
And when he'd eaten every state, each puppy, boy and girl
He wiped his mouth upon his sleeve and went to eat the world.

He ate the Egypt pyramids and every church in Rome,
And all the grass in Africa and all the ice in Nome.
He ate each hill in green Brazil and then to make things worse
He decided for dessert he'd eat the universe.

He started with the moon and stars and soon as he was done
He gulped the clouds, he sipped the wind and gobbled up the sun.
Then sitting there in the cold dark air,
He started to nibble his feet,
Then his legs, then his hips
Then his neck, then his lips
Till he sat there just gnashin' his teeth
'Cause nothin' was nothin' was
Nothin' was nothin' was
Nothin' was left to eat.

SHEL SILVERSTEIN

SQUISHY TOUCH

Everything King Midas touched
Turned to gold, the lucky fellow.
Every single thing I touch
Turns to raspberry Jell-O.
Today I touched the kitchen wall (squish),
I went and punched my brother Paul (splish).
I tried to fix my bike last week (sploosh),
And kissed my mother on the cheek (gloosh).

I got into my overshoes (sklush).
I tried to read the Evening News (smush),
I sat down in the easy chair (splush),
I tried to comb my wavy hair (slush).
I took a dive into the sea (glush) –
Would you like to shake hands with me (sklush)?

SHEL SILVERSTEIN

KIDNAPPED!

This morning I got kidnapped
By three masked men.
They stopped me on the sidewalk,
And offered me some candy,
And when I wouldn't take it
They grabbed me by the collar,
And pinned my arms behind me,
And shoved me in the backseat
Of this big black limousine and
Tied my hands behind my back
With sharp and rusty wire.
Then they put a blindfold on me
So I couldn't see where they took me,
And plugged up my ears with cotton
So I couldn't hear their voices.
And drove for 20 miles or

At least for 20 minutes, and then
Dragged me from the car down to
Some cold and moldy basement,
Where they stuck me in a corner
And went off to get the ransom
Leaving one of them to guard me
With a shotgun pointed at me,
Tied up sitting on a stool . . .
That's why I'm late for school!

SHEL SILVERSTEIN

FAIRY STORY

I went into the wood one day
And there I walked and lost my way

When it was so dark I could not see
A little creature came to me

He said if I would sing a song
The time would not be very long

But first I must let him hold my hand tight
Or else the wood would give me a fright

I sang a song, he let me go
But now I am home again there is nobody I know.

STEVIE SMITH

I HATE

I hate the way my mom calls me "Wend".
I've got nothing to do!
I've played all my games and read all my books –
What can I do?

I hate my Dad when he's buried in the paper.

"What can I do Dad?"
It's raining and it's cold, I can't go out –
What can I do?

I hate all these fish, when they gulp
Through the glass.
I've nothing to do!
All I can think of is to make faces back
– That's what I'll do.

WENDY SNAPE

THE INCHCAPE ROCK

No stir in the air, no stir in the sea;
The ship was still as she could be;
Her sails from heaven received no motion;
Her keel was steady in the ocean.

Without either sign or sound of their shock,
The waves flowed over the Inchcape Rock;
So little they rose, so little they fell,
They did not move the Inchcape Bell.

The worthy Abbot of Aberbrothok
Had placed that bell on the Inchcape Rock;
On a buoy in the storm it floated and swung,
And over the waves its warning rung.

When the rock was hid by the surge's swell,
The mariners heard the warning bell;
And then they knew the perilous rock,
And blest the Abbot of Aberbrothok.

The sun in heaven was shining gay,
All things were joyful on that day;
The sea birds screamed as they wheeled around,
And there was joyance in their sound.

The buoy of the Inchcape Bell was seen,
A darker speck on the ocean green.
Sir Ralph the Rover walked his deck,
And he fixed his eye on the darker speck.

He felt the cheering power of Spring;
It made him whistle; it made him sing;
His heart was mirthful to excess;
But the Rover's mirth was wickedness.

His eye was on the Inchcape float;
Quoth he, "My men, put out the boat,
And row me to the Inchcape Rock,
And I'll plague the Abbot of Aberbrothok."

The boat is lowered; the boatmen row,
And to the Inchcape Rock they go.
Sir Ralph bent over from the boat,
And he cut the bell from the Inchcape float.

Down sank the bell with a gurgling sound;
The bubbles rose and burst around.
Quoth Sir Ralph, "The next who comes to the Rock
Won't bless the Abbot of Aberbrothok."

Sir Ralph the Rover sailed away;
He scoured the seas for many a day;
And now, grown rich with plundered store,
He steers his course for Scotland's shore.

So thick a haze o'erspreads the sky
They cannot see the sun on high;
The wind hath blown a gale all day;
At evening it hath died away.

On deck the Rover takes his stand;
So dark it is they see no land.
Quoth Sir Ralph, "It will be lighter soon;
For there is the dawn of the rising moon."

"Canst hear," said one, "the breaker's roar?
For methinks we should be near the shore."
"Now where we are I cannot tell;
But I wish I could hear the Inchcape Bell!"

They hear no sound; the swell is strong;
Though the wind hath fallen they drift along,
Till the vessel strikes with a shivering shock, –
"Oh heavens! it is the Inchcape Rock!"

Sir Ralph the Rover tore his hair;
He cursed himself in his despair.
The waves rush in on every side;
The ship is sinking beneath the tide.

But even now, in his dying fear
One dreadful sound could the Rover hear –
A sound as if, with the Inchcape Bell,
The fiends in triumph were ringing his knell.

ROBERT SOUTHEY

THE BEE-KEEPER

The bee-keeper kissed me.
By the taste of honey I knew it was he.

SPANISH POEM
(translated by W. S. Merwin)

THERE WAS AN INDIAN

There was an Indian, who had known no change,
    Who strayed content along a sunlit beach
Gathering shells. He heard a sudden strange
    Commingled noise; looked up; and gasped for speech.
For in the bay, where nothing was before,
    Moved on the sea, by magic, huge canoes,
With bellying cloths on poles, and not one oar,
    And fluttering coloured signs and clambering crews.
And he, in fear, this naked man alone,
    His fallen hands forgetting all their shells,
His lips gone pale, knelt low behind a stone,
    And stared, and saw, and did not understand,
Columbus's doom-burdened caravels·
    Slant to the shore, and all their seamen land.

[= kind of sailing ship]

SIR JOHN SQUIRE

BLOCK CITY

What are you able to build with your blocks?
Castle and palaces, temples and docks.
Rain may keep raining, and others go roam,
But I can be happy and building at home.

Let the sofa be mountains, the carpet be sea,
There I'll establish a city for me:
A kirk· and a mill and a palace beside,
And a harbour as well where my vessels may ride.

[= church]

"Methought I saw a thousand fearful wracks; a thousand men that fishes gnawed upon." (p. 183)

Great is the palace with pillar and wall,
A sort of a tower on the top of it all,
And steps coming down in an orderly way
To where my toy vessels lie safe in the bay.

This one is sailing and that one is moored:
Hark to the song of the sailors on board!
And see on the steps of my palace, the kings
Coming and going with presents and things!

Now I have done with it, down let it go!
All in a moment the town is laid low.
Block upon block lying scattered and free,
What is there left of my town by the sea?

Yet as I saw it, I see it again,
The kirk and the palace, the ships and the men,
And as long as I live, and where'er I may be,
I'll always remember my town by the sea.

ROBERT LOUIS STEVENSON

ESCAPE AT BEDTIME

The lights from the parlour and kitchen shone out
    Through the blinds and the windows and bars;
And high overhead and all moving about,
    There were thousands of millions of stars.
There ne'er were such thousands of leaves on a tree,
    Nor of people in church or the Park,
As the crowds of the stars that looked down upon me,
    And that glittered and winked in the dark.

The Dog, and the Plough, and the Hunter, and all,
    And the star of the sailor, and Mars,
These shone in the sky, and the pail by the wall
    Would be half full of water and stars.

They saw me at last, and they chased me with cries,
    And they soon had me packed into bed;
But the glory kept shining and bright in my eyes,
    And the stars going round in my head.

ROBERT LOUIS STEVENSON

THE LAND OF STORY-BOOKS

At evening when the lamp is lit,
Around the fire my parents sit;
They sit at home and talk and sing,
And do not play at anything.

Now, with my little gun, I crawl
All in the dark along the wall,
And follow round the forest track
Away behind the sofa back.

There, in the night, where none can spy,
All in my hunter's camp I lie,
And play at books that I have read
Till it is time to go to bed.

These are the hills, these are the woods,
These are my starry solitudes;
And there the river by whose brink
The roaring lions come to drink.

I see the others far away
As if in firelit camp they lay,
And I, like to an Indian scout,
Around their party prowled about.

So, when my nurse comes in for me,
Home I return across the sea,
And go to bed with backward looks
At my dear land of Story-books.

ROBERT LOUIS STEVENSON

WINDY NIGHTS

Whenever the moon and stars are set,
  Whenever the wind is high,
All night long in the dark and wet,
  A man goes riding by.
Late in the night when the fires are out,
Why does he gallop and gallop about?

Whenever the trees are crying aloud,
  And ships are tossed at sea,
By, on the highway, low and loud,
  By at the gallop goes he.
By at the gallop he goes, and then
By he comes back at the gallop again.

ROBERT LOUIS STEVENSON

THE CLOUD-MOBILE

Above my face is a map
where continents form and fade.
Blue countries, made
on a white sea, are erased;
white countries are traced
on a blue sea.

It is a map that moves
faster than real
but so slow;
only my watching proves
that island has being,
or that bay.

It is a model of time;
mountains are wearing away,
coasts cracking, the ocean
spills over, then new
hills heap into view
with river-cuts of blue between them.

It is a map of change:
this is the way things are
with a stone or a star.
This is the way things go,
hard or soft,
swift or slow.

MAY SWENSON

196

THE EAGLE

He clasps the crag with crooked hands;
Close to the sun in lonely lands,
Ringed with the azure˙ world, he stands.   [= clear blue of the sky]

The wrinkled sea beneath him crawls;
He watches from his mountain walls,
And like a thunderbolt he falls.

LORD TENNYSON

MOTH

Filling a jug with hot water
I saw a black flutter,
saw something leap.
A moth danced on the scalding water.
In my childhood I tore wings off flies.
Now I can hear the screams of scalded moths.

D. M. THOMAS

THE MEWLIPS

The shadows where the Mewlips dwell
Are dark and wet as ink,
And slow and softly rings their bell,
As in the slime you sink.

You sink into the slime, who dare
To knock upon their door,
While down the grinning gargoyles stare
And noisome waters pour.

Beside the rotting river-strand
The drooping willows weep,
And gloomily the gorcrows stand
Croaking in their sleep.

Over the Merlock Mountains a long and weary way,
In a mouldy valley where the trees are grey,
By a dark pool's borders without wind or tide,
Moonless and sunless, the Mewlips hide.

The cellars where the Mewlips sit
Are deep and dank and cold
With single sickly candle lit;
And there they count their gold.

Their walls are wet, their ceilings drip;
Their feet upon the floor
Go softly with a squish-flap-flip,
As they sidle to the door.

They peep out slyly; through a crack
Their feeling fingers creep,
And when they've finished, in a sack
Your bones they take to keep.

Beyond the Merlock Mountains, a long and lonely road,
Through the spider-shadows and the marsh of Tode,
And through the wood of hanging trees and the gallows-weed,
You go to find the Mewlips – and the Mewlips feed.

J. R. R. TOLKIEN

THE DUCK AND THE MOON

A duck was once swimming along the river
looking for fish.
The whole day passed
without her finding a single one.
　　When night came
she saw the moon reflected on the water,
and thinking it was a fish
she dived down to catch it.
The other ducks saw her,
and they all made fun of her.
　　From that day
the duck was so ashamed and so timid,
that even when she did see a fish under water
she would not try to catch it,
and before long she died of hunger.

LEO TOLSTOY

THE RUINS OF LO-YANG

I climb to the ridge of Pei Mang Mountain
And look down on the city of Lo-yang.
In Lo-yang how still it is!
Palaces and houses all burnt to ashes.
Walls and fences all broken and gaping,
Thorns and brambles shooting up to the sky.
I do not see the old old-men:
I only see the new young men.

I turn aside, for the straight road is lost:
The fields are overgrown and will never be ploughed again.
I have been away such a long time
That I do not know which street is which.
How sad and ugly the empty moors are!
A thousand miles without the smoke of a chimney.
I think of the house I lived in all those years:
        I am heart-tied and cannot speak.

TS'AO CHIH
(translated by Arthur Waley)

THE MILKY WAY

My mother taught me that every night a procession of junks carrying lanterns moves silently across the sky, and the water sprinkled from their paddles falls to the earth in the form of dew. I no longer believe that the stars are junks carrying lanterns, no longer that the dew is shaken from their oars.

ALLEN UPWARD

MY PAPER ROUTE

When 3:30 or 4 o'clock comes around
It's like fresh roses
Because it's time to deliver my papers

It feels so good to meet my customers
and say hello
And then say goodbye

I deliver 81 papers during the week
So I hear 81 hellos
And 81 good byes

And 109 on Saturday.

TROY VACCIANO

MOUNT ETNA, A VOLCANO IN SICILY

There lies a safe beach, sheltered from all four winds; it is calm
And roomy too; but nearby, Etna thunderously erupts.
Again and again, it discharges at heaven a murky cloud,
a swirl of pitch-black smoke lurid with white-hot cinders,
And volleys of huge balls of flame, singeing the very stars.
Again and again, as if the mountain's guts were being coughed up,
it belches rocks, and groaning, vomits out thick streams
of lava, seething from its roots.

The story goes
That Enceladus, charred by Jove's lightning, is crushed beneath
this mountain mass – that Etna was dumped down bodily on him;
so, every time he turns over to rest one aching side,
Sicily quakes and rumbles, smoke hangs above like a great sheet.

VIRGIL
(translated by C. D. Lewis)

UPSTAIRS

I went upstairs
to watch it move.
I kept it there
under some clothes
in a small box.
It felt so warm
when I held it.
Then I dropped it.
It didn't move
for a long time.
And the next day
when I touched it,
it felt funny.
It wouldn't crawl.
It wasn't warm.
Something was bad

inside. I knew
it wasn't mine
the way it was.
It's still up there.
I don't want it
because it's cold.
I won't go near.
I stay downstairs.
It's warm down here
and I'm happy.

JOHN STEVENS WADE

LINEAGE

My grandmothers were strong.
They followed plows and bent to toil.
They moved through fields sowing seed.
They touched earth and grain grew.
They were full of sturdiness and singing.
My grandmothers were strong.

My grandmothers are full of memories
Smelling of soap and onions and wet clay
With veins rolling roughly over quick hands
They have many clean words to say.
My grandmothers were strong.
Why am I not as they?

MARGARET WALKER

THE SONG OF SNOHOMISH*

Catfish, Mudcat, Ducky, Coot.
The Babe, The Barber, The Blade, The Brat.
Windy, Dummy, Gabby, Hoot.
Big Train, Big Six, Big Ed, Fat.

Greasy, Sandy, Muddy, Rocky.
Bunions, Twinkletoes, Footsie, The Hat.
Fuzzy, Dizzy, Buddy, Cocky.
The Bull, The Stork, The Weasel, The Cat.

    Schoolboy, Preacher,
    Rajah, Duke,
    General, Major, Spaceman, Spook.

Shoeless Joe, Cobra Joe, Bullet Joe.
Bing.
Old Hoss, Mule, Country, Rube.
Smokey Joe, Fireman Joe, Jersey Joe.
Ping.
Bulldog, Squirrel, Puddin' Head, Boob.

The Georgia Peach, The Fordham Flash.
The Flying Dutchman, Cot.
The People's Cherce, The Blazer, Crash.
The Staten Island Scot.

    Skeeter, Scooter,
    Pepper, Duster,
    Ebba, Bama, Booms, Buster.

Three-Finger, No-Neck, The Knuck, The Lip.
Casey, Dazzy, Hippity, Zim.
Flit, Bad Henry, Fat Freddie, Flip.
Jolly Cholly, Sunny Jim.

Baby Doll, Angel Sleeves, Pep, Sliding Billy.
Buttercup, Bollicky, Boileryard, Juice,

* This poem is made up entirely of baseball players' nicknames.

Colby Jack, Dauntless Dave, Cheese, Gentle Willie,
Trolley Line, Wagon Tongue, Rough, What's the Use.

    Ee-yah,
    Poosh 'Em Up,
    Skoonj, Slats, Ski.
    Ding Dong,
    Ding-a-Ling,
    Dim Dom, Dee.

Bubbles, Dimples, Cuddles, Pinky.
Poison Ivy, Vulture, Stinky.

    Jigger, Jabbo
    Jolting Joe
    Blue Moon
    Boom Boom
    Bubba
    Bo.

WILLIAM S. WALLACE

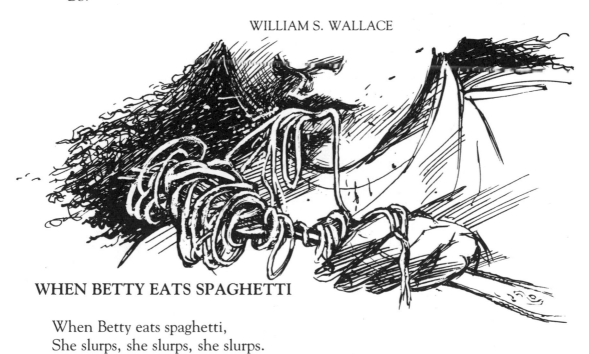

WHEN BETTY EATS SPAGHETTI

When Betty eats spaghetti,
She slurps, she slurps, she slurps.
And when she's finished slurping,
She burps, she burps, she burps.

COLIN WEST

THE RUNAWAY SLAVE

The runaway slave came to my house and stopt outside,
I heard his motions crackling the twigs of the woodpile,
Through the swung half-door of the kitchen I saw him limpsy and weak,
And went where he sat on a log and led him in and assured him,
And brought water and fill'd a tub for his sweated body and bruis'd feet,
And gave him a room that enter'd from my own, and gave him some
    coarse clean clothes,
And remember perfectly well his revolving eyes and his awkwardness,
And remember putting plasters on the galls of his neck and ankles;
He staid with me a week before he was recuperated and pass'd north.
I had him sit next me at table, my fire-lock lean'd in the corner.

WALT WHITMAN

THE COMMON QUESTION

Behind us at our evening meal
    The gray bird ate his fill,
Swung downward by a single claw
    And wiped his hookèd bill.

He shook his wings and crimson tail,
    And set his head aslant,
And, in his sharp, impatient way,
    Asked, "What does Charlie want?"

"Fie, silly bird!" I answered, "tuck
    Your head beneath your wing,
And go to sleep;" – but o'er and o'er
    He asked the self-same thing . . .

He shook his wings and crimson tail,
    And set his head aslant,
And, in his sharp, impatient way,
    Asked, "What does Charlie want?"

JOHN GREENLEAF WHITTIER

STAMPS

I collected stamps
Papa gave me a big bagful
I didn't collect stamps anymore

SIV WIDERBERG

NIGHTMARE

I never say his name aloud
and don't tell anybody
I always close all the drawers
and look behind the door before I go to bed
I cross my toes and count to eight
and turn the pillow over three times
Still he comes sometimes
one two three
like a shot
glaring at me with his eyes,
grating with his nails
and sneering his big sneer –
the Scratch Man

Oh-oh, now I said his name!
Mama, I can't sleep!

SIV WIDERBERG

PAPA

My papa can drive a car
My papa can fix electric motors
My papa can carry heavy, heavy things
My papa can quarrel with Uncle Carl
My papa can fry beef fried with onions

My papa can be kind
and comfort me when I cry

But can he cry himself?

I don't know

SIV WIDERBERG

HEAVEN

Up there amongst the clouds and suns
With melons and peaches and lots of buns
Where history books are out of date
And no one goes to bed till late –
That's the land to which I'll go
Where you push a button
And down comes snow

CHINA WILLIAMS

"The cellars where the Mewlips sit are deep and dank and cold." (p. 199)

THE LAST WORDS OF MY ENGLISH GRANDMOTHER

1920
There were some dirty plates
and a glass of milk
beside her on a small table
near the rank, disheveled bed –

Wrinkled and nearly blind
she lay and snored
rousing with anger in her tones
to cry for food,

Gimme something to eat –
They're starving me –
I'm all right I won't go
to the hospital. No, no, no

Give me something to eat
Let me take you
to the hospital, I said
and after you are well

you can do as you please.
She smiled, Yes
you do what you please, first
then I can do what I please –

Oh, oh, oh! she cried
as the ambulance men lifted
her to the stretcher –
Is this what you call

making me comfortable?
By now her mind was clear –
Oh you think you're smart
you young people,

she said, but I'll tell you
you don't know anything.
Then we started.

On the way

we passed a long row
of elms. She looked at them
awhile out of
the ambulance window and said,

What are all those
fuzzy-looking things out there?
Trees? Well, I'm tired
of them and rolled her head away.

WILLIAM CARLOS WILLIAMS

THE TERM

A rumpled sheet
of brown paper
about the length

and apparent bulk
of a man was
rolling with the

wind slowly over
and over in
the street as

a car drove down
upon it and
crushed it to

the ground. Unlike
a man it rose
again rolling

with the wind over
and over to be as
it was before.

WILLIAM CARLOS WILLIAMS

SUZANNE

Brother Paul! look!
– but he rushes to a different
window.
The moon!

I heard shrieks and thought:
What's that?

That's just Suzanne
talking to the moon!
Pounding on the window
with both fists:

      Paul!   Paul!

– and talking to the moon.
Shrieking
and pounding the glass
with both fists!

Brother Paul! the moon!

WILLIAM CARLOS WILLIAMS

OLD MAN TRAVELLING
(Animal Tranquillity And Decay, – A Sketch)

The little hedge-row birds,
That peck along the road, regard him not.
He travels on, and in his face, his step,
His gait, is one expression; every limb,
His look and bending figure, all bespeak
A man who does not move with pain, but moves
With thought – He is insensibly subdued
To settled quiet: he is one by whom
All effort seems forgotten, one to whom
Long patience has such mild composure given,
That patience now doth seem a thing, of which
He hath no need. He is by nature led
To peace so perfect, that the young behold
With envy, what the old man hardly feels.
– I asked him whither he was bound, and what
The object of his journey; he replied
"Sir! I am going many miles to take
A last leave of my son, a mariner,
Who from a sea-fight has been brought to Falmouth,
And there is dying in an hospital."

WILLIAM WORDSWORTH

FLOOD YEAR

Walking up the driftwood beach at day's end
I saw it, thrust up out of a hillock of sand –
a frail bleached clench of fingers dried by wind –
the dead child's hand.

And they are mourning there still, though I forget,
the year of flood, the scoured ruined land,
the herds gone down the current, the farms drowned,
and the child never found.

When I was there the thick hurling waters
had gone back to the river, the farms were almost drained.
Banished half-dead cattle searched the dunes; it rained;
river and sea met with a wild sound.

Oh with a wild sound water flung into air
where sea met river; all the country round
no heart was quiet. I walked on the driftwood sand
and saw the pale crab crouched, and came to a stand
thinking, A child's hand. The child's hand.

JUDITH WRIGHT

SERGEANT BROWN'S PARROT

Many policemen wear upon their shoulders
cunning little radios. To pass away the time
They talk about the traffic to them, listen to the news,
And it helps them to Keep Down Crime

But Sergeant Brown, he wears upon his shoulder
A tall green parrot as he's walking up and down
And all the parrot says is "Who's a-pretty-boy-then?"
"I am," says Sergeant Brown.

KIT WRIGHT

QUICKSTEP

Way down Geneva,
All along Vine,
Deeper than the snowdrift
Love's eyes shine:

Mary Lou's walking
In the winter time.

She's got

Red boots on, she's got
Red boots on,
Kicking up the winter
Till the winter's gone.

So

Go by Ontario,
Look down Main,
If you can't Mary Lou
Come back again:

Sweet light burning
In winter's flame.

She's got

Snow in her eyes, got
A tingle in her toes
And new red boots on
Wherever she goes.

So

All around Lake Street,
Up by St. Paul,
Quicker than the white wind
Love takes all:

Mary Lou's walking
In the big snow fall.

She's got

Red boots on, she's got
Red boots on,
Kicking up the winter
Till the winter's gone.

KIT WRIGHT

TO A SQUIRREL AT KYLE-NA-NO

Come play with me;
Why should you run
Through the shaking tree
As though I'd a gun
To strike you dead?
When all I would do
Is to scratch your head
And let you go.

W. B. YEATS

215

HIGHWAYMAN'S HOLLOW

"Where the cliff hangs hollow, where the gloom falls chill,
You hear a something, follow, follow, follow down the hill;
Where the horses sweat and lather and the dusk begins to gather
It is there that I will meet you and will greet you,
      You, Sir Traveller."

"Where the leaves lie rotting and the night falls blind,
You hear a someone trotting, trotting, trotting down the wind,
And you listen all a-shiver to my ghostly 'Stand, deliver,'
Yes, although my bones have whitened, you are frightened
      Yet, Sir Traveller."

" 'Twas a traveller who slew me where the dark firs frown,
'Twas his small sword through me and the blood dripped down.
Where the horses sweat and lather and the dusk begins to gather,
It is there I ride behind you to remind you,
      You, Sir Traveller."

GILBERT V. YONGE

LEOPARD

Gentle hunter
His tail plays on the ground
While he crushes the skull.

Beautiful death
Who puts on a spotted robe
When he goes to his victim.

Playful killer
Whose loving embrace
Splits the antelope's heart.

YORUBA POEM

MOSQUITO

Mozzie

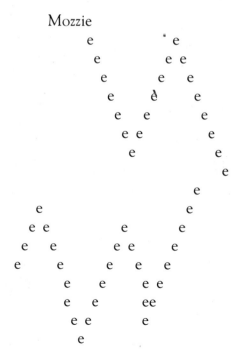

MARIE ZBIERSKI

217

BALLADS
(all Anon.)

DUNDERBECK

Oh, Dunderbeck, oh Dunderbeck,
How could you be so mean,
To ever have invented
The sausage meat machine?
Now long-tailed rats and pussy-cats
Will never more be seen,
They'll all be ground to sausage meat
In Dunderbeck's machine.

One day a little fat boy came
Walking in the store,
He bought a pound of sausages
And laid them on the floor.
Then he began to whistle,
He whistled up a tune,
The sausages, they jumped, they barked,
They danced 'round the room. Bang!

One day the thing got busted,
The darn thing wouldn't go,
And Dunderbeck he crawled inside
To see what made it so.
His wife came walking in just then,
From shopping in the street,
She brushed against the starting rod
And Dunderbeck was meat! Bang!

218

WE SHALL NOT BE MOVED

We shall not, we shall not be moved,
We shall not, we shall not be moved,
Just like a tree that's standing by the water,
We shall not be moved.

HOW COMES THAT BLOOD?

"How comes that blood all over your shirt?
My son, come tell it to me."
"It's the blood of my little guinea pig –
O mother, please let me be."

"Your guinea pig's blood is not so red.
My son, come tell it to me."
"It's the blood of my little hunting dog
That played in the field for me . . ."

"Your dog lies yonder, O my son,
And this it could not be."
"It is the blood of my old roan horse
That pulled the plow for me . . ."

"How comes that blood all over your shirt?
My son, you must tell to me."
"It's the blood of my little brother Bill
Who I killed in the field today . . ."

"And what will you do when your father comes home?
My son, come tell it to me."
"I'll put my feet in the bottom of a boat
And sail across the sea."

THE WILD HOG

There is a wild hog in the wood,
He kills the men and drinks their blood.

There he comes through yonders marsh,
He splits his way through oak and ash.

Bangum drew his wooden knife,
To rob that wild hog of his life.

They fought four hours of the day,
At length that wild hog stole away.

They followed that wild hog to his den,
And there they found the bones of a thousand men.

THE FEMALE HIGHWAYMAN

Priscilla on one summer's day
Dressed herself up in men's array;
With a brace of pistols by her side
All for to meet her true love she did ride.

And when she saw her true love there
She boldly bade him for to stand.
"Stand and deliver, kind sir," she said,
"For if you don't I'll shoot you dead."

And when she'd robbed him of all his store,
Said she, "Kind sir, there's one thing more;
The diamond ring I've seen you wear,
Deliver that and your life I'll spare."

"That ring," said he, "my true love gave;
My life I'll lose but that I'll save."
Then, being tender-hearted like a dove,
She rode away from the man she love.

Anon they walked upon the green,
And he spied his watch pinned to her clothes,
Which made her blush, which made her blush
Like a full, blooming rose.

" 'Twas me who robbed you on the plain,
So here's your watch and your gold again.
I did it only for to see
If you would really faithful be.
And now I'm sure that this is true,
I also give my heart to you."

LADY ISABEL AND THE ELF KNIGHT

There was a man out in the land
 Who courted the maiden fair,
And promised to take her out to the North land
 And there their marriage should be.

Says, "Get some of your father's gold
 And some of your mother's feed,
And two the best horses that stands in the stall,
 That stands by forty and three."

221

She got some of her father's gold
  And some of her mother's feed,
And two the best horses that stood in the stall,
  That stood by forty and three.

She mounted all on her milky white horse
  And led her dapple grey,
And rode till she came to the great salt sea,
  Three hours before it was day.

"Dismount, dismount your milky white horse,
  Deliver them unto me,
For six pretty maidens I drownded here,
  And the seventh one you shall be.

"Take off, take off your silky white clothes
  And deliver them unto me,
For they are too great, too grand, too rich,
  To rock in this great salt sea."

"If I must take off my silky white clothes,
  Please turn your back on me,
For I think it not fit, for as often as you,
  An undressed lady to see."

He turned his back all unto her,
  And she wept bitterly.
She grabbed him around his waist so small
  And tumbled him into the sea.

He waved, oh, high, and he waved, oh, low,
  And waved till he came to her side.
"Take hold my hand, my pretty Polly,
  And you shall be my bride."

"Lie there, lie there, you horrid old wretch,
  Lie there, lie there," said she,
"For six pretty maidens you drownded in there,
  And the seventh one drownded you'll be."

She mounted all on her milky white horse
  And led her dapple grey
And rode till she came to her father's house
  One hour before it was day.

A parrot being up in his cage so high
  And unto her did say,
"What is the matter, my pretty Polly,
  You tarry so long before day?"

"Hold your tongue, hold your tongue, my pretty parrot,
  Don't tell no tales on me.
Your cage shall be lined with glittering gold
  And the doors with ivory."

The father being up at his window so high
  And unto her did say,
"What is the matter, my pretty parrot,
  You tarry so long before day?"

"There's matter enough," the parrot replies,
  "There's matter enough," said she.
"Two cats have been up in my cage so high,
  And I'm afraid they will catch me."

FRANKIE AND JOHNNY

Frankie and Johnny were lovers, O lordy how they could love.
Swore to be true to each other, true as the stars above;
He was her man, but he done her wrong.

Frankie she was his woman, everybody knows.
She spent one hundred dollars for a suit of Johnny's clothes.
He was her man, but he done her wrong.

Frankie and Johnny went walking, Johnny in his bran' new suit,
"O good Lawd," says Frankie, "but don't my Johnny look cute?"
He was her man, but he done her wrong.

Frankie went down to Memphis; she went on the evening train.
She paid one hundred dollars for Johnny a watch and chain.
He was her man, but he done her wrong.

Frankie went down to the corner, to buy a glass of beer;
She says to the fat bartender, "Has my loving man been here?
He was my man, but he done me wrong."

"Lady Isabel and the elf knight." (p. 221)

"Ain't going to tell you no story, ain't going to tell you no lie,
I seen your man 'bout an hour ago with a girl named Alice Bly –
If he's your man, he's doing you wrong."

Frankie went back to the hotel, she didn't go there for fun,
Under her long red kimono she toted a forty-four gun.
He was her man, but he done her wrong.

Frankie went down to the hotel, looked in the window so high,
There was her lovin' Johnny a-lovin' up Alice Bly;
He was her man, but he done her wrong.

Frankie went down to the hotel, she rang that hotel bell,
"Stand back all of you floozies or I'll blow you all to hell,
I want my man, he's doin' me wrong."

Frankie threw back her kimono; took out the old forty-four;
Roota-toot-toot, three times she shot, right through that hotel door.
She shot her man, 'cause he done her wrong.

Johnny grabbed off his Stetson. "O good Lawd, Frankie, don't shoot."
But Frankie put her finger on the trigger, and the gun went roota-toot-
    toot.
He was her man, but she shot him down.

"Roll me over easy, roll me over slow,
Roll me over easy, boys, 'cause my wounds are hurting me so,
I was her man, but I done her wrong."

With the first shot Johnny staggered; with the second shot he fell;
When the third bullet hit him, there was a new man's face in hell.
He was her man, but he done her wrong.

Frankie heard a rumbling away down under the ground.
Maybe it was Johnny where she had shot him down.
He was her man, and she done him wrong.

"Oh, bring on your rubber-tired hearses, bring on your rubber-tired
    hacks,
They're takin' my Johnny to the buryin' groun' but they'll never bring
    him back.
He was my man, but he done me wrong."

The judge he said to the jury, "It's plain as plain can be.
This woman shot her man, so it's murder in the second degree.
He was her man, though he done her wrong."

Now it wasn't murder in the second degree, it wasn't murder in the
    third.
Frankie simply dropped her man, like a hunter drops a bird.
He was her man, but he done her wrong.

"Oh, put me in that dungeon. Oh, put me in that cell.
Put me where the northeast wind blows from the southeast corner of
    hell.
I shot my man 'cause he done me wrong."

Frankie walked up to the scaffold, as calm as a girl could be,
She turned her eyes to heaven and said, "Good Lord, I'm coming to
    thee.
He was my man, and I done him wrong."

ON THE BIRTH OF THE PRINCE OF WALES*

There's a pretty fuss and bother both in country and in town,
Since we have got a present, and an heir unto the Crown,
A little Prince of Wales so charming and so sly,
And the ladies shout with wonder, What a pretty little boy!

He must have a little musket, a trumpet and a kite,
A little penny rattle, and silver sword so bright,
A little cap and feather with scarlet coat so smart,
And a pretty little hobby horse to ride about the park.

He will want a little fiddle, and a little German flute,
A little pair of stockings and a pretty pair of boots,
With a handsome pair of spurs, and a golden headed cane,
And a stick of barley sugar, as long as Drury Lane.

Now to get these little niceties the taxes must be rose,
For the little Prince of Wales wants so many suits of clothes,
So they must tax the frying pan, the windows and the doors,
The bedsteads and the tables, kitchen pokers, and the floors.

*who was born on Tuesday, November 9, 1841

Limericks

A sleeper from the Amazon
Put nighties of his gra'mazon –
    The reason: That
    He was too fat
To get his own pajamazon.

There once was a damsel named Jinx,
Who when asked what she thought of the Sphinx,
    Replied with a smile,
    "That old fraud by the Nile?
I personally think that she stinks."

There was an old man of Nantucket
Who kept all his cash in a bucket;
    But his daughter, named Nan,
    Ran away with a man,
And as for the bucket, Nantucket.

A mosquito was heard to complain
That a chemist had poisoned his brain;
    The cause of his sorrow
    Was Para-dichloro-
Diphenyltrichlorothane.

A fly and a flea in a flue
Were imprisoned, so what could they do?
    Said the fly, "Let us flee!"
    "Let us fly!" said the flea,
So they flew through a flaw in the flue.

P. L. MANNOCK

228

A rare old bird is the Pelican,
His beak holds more than his belican.
    He can take in his beak
    Enough food for a week.
I'm darned if I know how the helican!

        DIXON MERRITT

There was an old man of St. Bees,
Who was stung in the arm by a wasp,
    When asked, "Does it hurt?"
    He replied, "No, it doesn't,
I'm so glad it wasn't a hornet."

        W. S. GILBERT

There was a young lady of Crewe
Who wanted to catch the 2.02.
    Said a porter, "Don't worry,
    Or hurry, or scurry,
It's a minute or two to 2.02."

A thrifty young fellow of Shoreham
Made brown paper trousers and woreham;
    He looked nice and neat
    Till he bent in the street
To pick up a pin; then he toreham.

There was a young lady of Twickenham
Whose shoes were too tight to walk quick in 'em.
    She came back from a walk
    Looking whiter than chalk
And took 'em both off and was sick in 'em.

        OLIVER HERFORD

RIDDLES IN RHYME

This thing all things devours:
Birds, beasts, trees, flowers;
Gnaws iron, bites steel;
Grinds hard stones to meal;
Slays kings, ruins town,
And beats high mountains down.
A. *Time*

J. R. R. TOLKIEN

I fly –
like a bird,
And buzz –
like a bee,
Got a tail –
like a fish,
Got a hop –
like a flea.
A. *Helicopter*

A skin have I,
More eyes than one.
I can be nice when I am done.
A. *Potato*

On the way a miracle: water become bone.
A. *Icicle*

KEVIN CROSSLEY-HOLLAND
(Anglo-Saxon)

A large tree on which there are four branches,
Thirteen nests in every branch,
Seven eggs in every nest,
And twenty-four spots on every egg.
A. *The year with seasons, weeks per season, days, and hours.*

You use it between your head and toes,
The more it works the thinner it grows.
A. *Bar of soap*

Ten men's length
And ten men's strength
And ten men cannot set it on end.
A. *Rope*

Four fingers and a thumb
Yet flesh and bone have I none.
A. *Glove*

There was a farmer,
his lion
a bundle of hay
and a goat.
And they all wanted to cross the river.
If he left the goat with the lion
and took the hay first,
the lion would eat the goat.
If he left the hay there,
the goat would eat the hay.
So what could he do?
How could he take them across?
If he took the goat across,
the lion wouldn't eat the hay.
So he took the goat across,
came back,

took the hay
brought the goat back
took the lion
and then he came back
and took the goat back.

THE WILL

There was an old man who had three sons
And seventeen horses. "I've written my will,"
He told his sons. "I'm going to leave
My horses to the three of you.
But you must share them as I say."

The old man died. The will was opened:
"To my three sons I leave
My seventeen horses.
My eldest son shall take half;
My second son shall take a third;
My youngest son shall take a ninth.
    Shed no blood,
    Do not kill;
    You must obey
    Your father's will."

The three sons were puzzled. At school
They'd been well taught, but not so well
That they could divide
    17 by 2,
            17 by 3,
                    17 by 9,
And still obey their father's will.

What did they do?

They went to a wise man and asked
His advice. "I will give you a horse,"
Said the wise man. "Now go away
And obey your father's will."

232

They took the horse and went away.

They now had eighteen horses.
The eldest son took half;
The second son took a third;
The youngest son took a ninth.
And the wise man's horse? They gave it back.

Why did the old man write his will like that?

IAN SERRAILLIER

I am the terror of mankind,
My breath is flame, and by its power
I urge my messenger to find
A way into the strongest tower.
A. *Cannon.* A

Nonsense verse

Order in the court
The judge is eating beans
His wife is in the bath tub
Shooting submarines.

Dictation, dictation, dictation,
Three sausages went to the station,
One got lost
And one got squashed
And one had an operation.

I remember – I remember well –
The first girl that I kissed.
She closed her eyes, I closed mine,
And then – worst luck – we missed!

See you later, alligator.
In a while, crocodile.
See you later, hot potato.
If you wish, jelly-fish.
Not too soon, you big baboon.
Toodle-oo, kangaroo.
Bye-bye, butterfly.
See you tomorrow, horror.
In a week, freak.

Adam and Eve
In the Garden of Eden
Admiring the Beauties of Nature,
The Devil jumped out
Of a Brussels sprout
And hit 'em in the eye with a potato.

BUSY STREET

Sausage dog
Busy street
Motor car
Mince meat.

A peanut sat on the railroad track,
His heart was all a-flutter.
Along came a train –
Toot-toot! – peanut butter! *

The owner of the Inside Inn
Was outside his Inside Inn,
With his inside outside his Inside Inn.

Teacher, teacher don't be dumb
Give me back my bubble gum.
Teacher, teacher I declare
Tarzan lost his underwear.
Teacher, teacher, don't be mean
Give us a dime for the coke machine.

*Alternative last line "It went by" (Hughie's version).

235

I was looking back
To see if she was looking back
To see if I was looking back
To see if she was looking back at me.

Roses are red,
Violets are blue,
I have a boyfriend,
And so do you.
Tell your mum to hold her tongue
'Cause she had one when she was young.
Tell your dad to do the same
'Cause he was the one who changed your mum's name.

Row, row, row your boat
Gently down the stream,
If you see the crocodile,
Don't forget to scream.

Look at that bunch of cows.
Not bunch. Herd.
Heard of what?
Herd of cows.
Sure I've heard of cows.
No a cow-herd.
Why should I care what a cow heard?
I've got no secrets from a cow.

Don't look at me in that tone of voice
Or I'll deafen your eyesight.
Don't look at me in that tone of voice
It smells a funny colour.

HERE LIES:

Here lies a famous escapologist
Who was buried on the 19th, 20th,
And then again on the 21st June.

Sam, Sam, the butcher man,
Washed his face in a frying pan,
Combed his hair with a wagon wheel,
And died with a toothache in his heel.

Beneath this stone our baby lies,
He neither cries nor hollers;
He lived on earth just twenty days,
And cost us forty dollars.

Here lies John Bun,
He was killed by a gun.
His name was not Bun, but Wood,
But Wood would not rhyme with Gun,
* but Bun would.*

If I am so quickly done for
What on earth was I begun for?

He passed the bobby without any fuss,
And he passed the cart of hay,
He tried to pass a swerving bus,
And then he passed away.

Poor little Johnny
We'll never see him more –
For what he thought was H_2O
was H_2SO_4.

There's this man
he's in a room
there's no windows
no chimney
no door
nothing but a table.
So he got his hand
and chopped the table in half.
Two halves make a whole –
he crept through the hole
shouted down the hole
made himself hoarse
got on the horse
and galloped off.

SAY THESE THREE AS QUICK AS YOU CAN

Are you the guy
that told the guy
that I'm the guy
who gave the guy
the black eye?

No, I'm not the guy
who told the guy
that you're the guy
who gave the guy
the black eye.

Says she to me, "Was that you?"
Says I, "Who?"
Says she, "You."
Says I, "Where?"
Says she, "There."
Says I, "When?"
Says she, "Then."
Says I, "No."
Says she, "Oh . . ."

You remind me of a man
What man?
a man of power
what power?
the power of hoodoo
Who do?
You do
Do what?

LIDES TO BARY JADE (MARY JANE)

The bood is beabig brighdly love,
The sdars are shidig too;
While I ab gazig dreabily
Add thigkig, love, of you;
You caddot, oh, you caddot kdow,
By darlig, how I biss you –
(Oh, whadt a fearful cold I've got –
Ck-*tish*-u! Ck-ck-*tish*-u!)

WHAT SOME PEOPLE DO

Jibber, jabber, gabble, babble,
Cackle, clack and prate,
Twiddle, twaddle, mutter, stutter,
Utter, splutter, blate . . .

Chatter, patter, tattle, prattle,
Chew the rag and crack,
Spiel and spout and spit it out,
Tell the world and quack . . .

Sniffle, snuffle, drawl and bawl,
Snicker, snort and snap,
Bark and buzz and yap and yelp,
Chin and chirp and chat . . .

Shout and shoot and gargle, gasp,
Gab and gag and groan,
Hem and haw and work the jaw,
Grumble, mumble, moan . . .

Beef and bellyache and bat,
Say a mouthful, squawk,
That is what some people do
When they merely talk.

BOASTS

I know a man who's so strong
he can knock you up into the air so high
that you'll starve coming down

*I know a man who can run so fast
he meets himself coming back*

It's so hot round here
you can fry a steak to cinders
on a cake of ice

*I know a train that goes so fast
it reaches the station before its whistle*

I know a man who's so good at jumping
that he can jump across a river
and back
without touching the other side.

*It's so healthy round here
you have to shoot a man to start a graveyard*

The streets are so narrow round here
that the dogs wag their tails up and down

*It's so dry round here
we have to plant onions
in between the rows of potatoes
and then scratch the onions
to make the potato's eyes water enough
to sprinkle the rest of the garden*

I know a man who's so mean
he sends back his sausage skins to the butchers
to have them refilled

"When the third bullet hit him, there was a new man's face in hell." (p. 225)

I'm so hungry
my belly thinks my throat's been cut

The corn grows so fast round here
I asked my brother to sit on it
to stunt the growth
So he did
The next day he dropped me a note
"Passed through heaven yesterday
at twelve o'clock selling popcorn
to the angels"

It's so windy round here
you go out
you get blown against the wall and flattened out as wafers
they peel you off the walls
and sell you off as circus posters

There's a man round here
who is so tall
he has to climb a ladder to shave himself
when he was born he was so big
it was impossible to name all of him at once
he grew so fast
his head grew three inches through the top of his hat

I know two fellows
who are so lazy
it takes two of them to chop wood
one swings the axe
the other grunts

I know a man who's so forgetful
that one night he put his cat to bed
and put himself outside

(Collected from various sources by Michael Rosen)

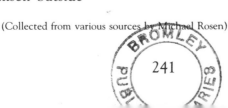
BROMLEY PUBLIC LIBRARIES

ACKNOWLEDGEMENTS

The editor and publishers gratefully acknowledge permission to reproduce the following copyright material:

Frederick d'Aguiar: 'Mama Dot Learns to Fly' from *Mama Dot* by Frederick d'Aguiar. Reprinted by permission of Chatto and Windus. Allan Ahlberg: 'The Cane' from Allan Ahlberg: *Please Mrs Butler* (Kestrel Books 1983) pp. 58–60. Copyright © 1983 by Allan Ahlberg. Reprinted by permission of Penguin Books Ltd. Dorothy Aldis: 'Wasps' by Dorothy Aldis reprinted by permission of G. P. Putnam's Sons from *Is Anybody Hungry?* by Dorothy Aldis, text copyright © 1964 by Dorothy Aldis. Al-Khansa: 'The Night'. Reprinted by permission of Schocken Books Inc. from *A Book of Women Poets From Antiquity to Now* by Aliki Barnstone and Willis Barnstone. Copyright © 1980 by Schocken Books Inc. W. H. Auden: 'Night Mail' from W. H. Auden: *Collected Poems*, edited by Edward Mendelson. 'Roman Wall Blues' from W. H. Auden: *Collected Poems*, edited by Edward Mendelson. Copyright 1940 and renewed 1968 by W. H. Auden. 'O What Is That Sound' from W. H. Auden: *Collected Poems*, edited by Edward Mendelson. Copyright 1937 and renewed 1965 by W. H. Auden. Reprinted by permission of Faber and Faber Ltd. and Random House Inc. Ilona Baburka: 'Dream'. Copyright © 1970 by Kenneth Koch. Joan Batchelor: 'I Saw a Sad Man in a Field'. Reprinted by permission of the author. Hilaire Belloc: 'Tarantella' from *Complete Verse*. Reprinted by permission of Gerald Duckworth and Co. Ltd. and A. D. Peters and Co. Ltd. John Betjeman: 'On a Portrait of a Deaf Man' from *Collected Poems*. Reprinted by permission of John Murray Publishers Ltd. Alan Brownjohn: 'After Prevert' from *Collected Poems 1952–83*. Reprinted by permission of Martin Secker and Warburg Ltd. Ian Campbell: 'The Sun is Burning'. Copyright © 1963 TRO Essex Music Ltd. of 7 Bury Place, London WC1A 2LA, for the World. International Copyright Secured. All Rights Reserved. Used By Permission. Catullus: 'I Hate and I Love' Poem No. 85 from *The Poems of Catullus*, translated by Peter Whigham (Penguin Classics 1966) p. 197. This translation and introduction copyright © Peter Whigham, 1966. Reprinted by permission of Penguin Books Ltd. Charles Causley: 'What Has Happened to Lulu?' from *Figgie Hobbin* (Macmillan). Reprinted by permission of David Higham Associates Ltd. Geoffrey Chaucer: 'The Miller's Tale' from *The Canterbury Tales*, translated by Nevill Coghill. Copyright 1951 by Nevill Coghill. Copyright © Nevill Coghill, 1958, 1960, 1975, 1977. Reprinted by permission of Penguin Books Ltd. Sharon Cheeks: 'Stretching' from *Cadbury's Second Selection of Children's Poetry*. Reprinted by permission of Cadbury Schweppes. Ian Crichton Smith: 'The Nose (after Gogol)' from *In the Middle*. Reprinted by permission of Victor Gollancz Ltd. e. e. cummings: 'maggie and millie and molly and may'. Copyright © 1956 by e. e. cummings. Reprinted from his volume *Complete Poems 1913–1962* by permission of Harcourt Brace Jovanovich Inc. and from *Complete Poems 1910–1962* by permission of Granada Publishing Ltd. 'Buffalo Bill's' published in the UK in e. e. cummings: *The Complete Poems 1910–1962* and in the US in *Tulips and Chimneys* copyright 1923, 1925 and renewed 1951, 1953 by e. e. cummings. Copyright © 1973, 1976 by The Trustees for the e. e. cummings Trust. Copyright © 1973, 1976 by George James Firmage. Reprinted by permission of Granada Publishing Ltd. and Liveright Publishing Corporation. Andrew Darlington: 'Think Carefully Before Reading This'. Reprinted by permission of Faber and Faber Ltd. from *Hard Lines: New Poetry and Prose*. Idris Davies: 'The Miner' (stanza VII) from *Gwalia Deserta*. Reprinted by permission of Ebenezer Morris. Jan Dean: 'Writing' from *What's In a Poem*, edited by B. Boyle. Reprinted by permission of the author. Walter de la Mare: 'Peeping Tom'. Reprinted by permission of The Literary Trustees of Walter de la Mare and The Society of Authors as their representative. Richard Digance: 'The Turkey' and 'The Bear' from *Animal Alphabet*. Reprinted by permission of Michael Joseph Ltd. Hilda Doolittle (H.D.): 'Heat' from H.D.: *Collected Poems 1912–1944*. Copyright © 1982 by the Estate of Hilda Doolittle. Reprinted by permission of New Directions Publishing Corporation. Bob Dylan: 'Who Killed Davey Moore?' © 1964 Warner Bros. Inc. All Rights Reserved. Used By Permission. William Eastlake: 'The Space Program' from *A Child's Garden of Verses for the Revolution*. Reprinted by permission of the author. T. S. Eliot: 'Skimbleshanks: The Railway Cat' from *Old Possum's Book of Practical Cats* by T. S. Eliot. Copyright 1939 by T. S. Eliot; renewed 1967 by Esme Valerie Eliot. 'Preludes' from *Collected Poems 1909–1962* by T. S. Eliot. Copyright 1936 by Harcourt Brace Jovanovich, Inc., copyright © 1963, 1964 by T. S. Eliot. Reprinted by permission of Faber and Faber Ltd. and Harcourt Brace Jovanovich, Inc. D. J. Enright: 'The Old Field' from *Rhyme Times Rhyme* (Chatto and Windus). Reprinted by permission of Watson Little Ltd. Willard R. Espy: 'Private? No!' and 'What's Its Name' from *Another Almanac of Words at Play* (1980). Reprinted by permission of Andre Deutsch Ltd. 'What's Its Name?' Reprinted from *Another Almanac of Words at Play* by Willard R. Espy. Copyright © 1980 by Willard R. Espy. Used by permission of Clarkson N. Potter, Inc. Lawrence Ferlinghetti: 'Summer in Brooklyn' from *A Coney Island of the Mind*. Copyright 1958 by Lawrence Ferlinghetti. Reprinted by permission of New Directions Publishing Corporation. Frank Flynn: 'Spaghetti' © Frank Flynn 1984/Reprinted from *The Candy-floss Tree*: poems by Gerda Mayer, Frank Flynn, and Norman Nicholson (1984) by permission of Oxford University Press. Robert Froman: 'Superstink' and 'Friendly Warning'. Reprinted by permission of the author. Robert Frost: 'The Road Not Taken' from *The Poetry of Robert Frost*, edited by Edward Connery Lathem. Reprinted by permission of the Estate of Robert Frost, Jonathan Cape Ltd. and Holt Rinehart and Winston. James

Godden: 'Lost' from *Slowly But Surely*. Reprinted by permission of EMI Music Publishing Ltd. Seamus Heaney: 'The Railway Children' from *Station Island* by Seamus Heaney. Copyright © 1985 by Seamus Heaney. Reprinted by permission of Faber and Faber Ltd. and Farrar, Straus and Giroux Inc. John Hegley: 'Children With Adults' from *Apples and Snakes*. Reprinted by permission of the author. A. P. Herbert: 'The Spider'. Reprinted by permission of Lady Herbert. Mary Ann Hoberman: 'Yellow Butter'. Copyright © 1978 by Mary Ann Hoberman. Reprinted by permission of Russell and Volkening, Inc. as agents for the author. Lucy Hosegood: 'Starlings' from *Those First Affections*, edited by T. Rogers. Reprinted by permission of Routledge and Kegan Paul. Langston Hughes: 'Madam and her Madam'. Copyright 1948 by Alfred A. Knopf, Inc. Reprinted from *Selected Poems of Langston Hughes* by permission of Alfred A. Knopf, Inc. Ted Hughes: 'There Came a Day' from *Season Songs* by Ted Hughes. Copyright © 1968, 1973, 1975 by Ted Hughes. Reprinted by permission of Faber and Faber Ltd. and Viking Penguin Inc. James Hurley: 'Greedy Dog'. Reprinted by permission of the author. Nana Issaia: 'Dream', translated by Helle Tzaopoulou Barnstone, from *A Book of Women Poets*. Reprinted by permission of Helle Tzaopoulou Barnstone. David Jackson: 'Irritating Sayings' from *Ways of Talking*, edited by David Jackson. Reprinted by permission of Ward Lock Educational Co. Ltd. Karen Jackson: 'All For An Ice-cream' from *Ways of Talking*, edited by David Jackson. Reprinted by permission of Ward Lock Educational Co. Ltd. Teresa de Jésus: 'It Makes Me Furious!'. Reprinted by permission of Curbstone. Carolyn Kizer: 'Through a Glass Eye, Lightly' from *Mermaids in the Basement: Poems for Women* (Copper Canyon Press). Reprinted by permission of the author. John Lennon and Paul Macartney: 'I'm Only Sleeping'. Reprinted by permission of ATV Music. Vachel Lindsay: 'The Little Turtle'. Reprinted with permission of Macmillan Publishing Company from *Collected Poems* by Vachal Lindsay. Copyright 1920 by Macmillan Publishing Co., Inc. renewed 1948 by Elizabeth C. Lindsay. Christopher Logue: 'London Airport' from *Ode to the Dodo*. Reprinted by permission of Jonathan Cape Ltd. and the Tessa Sayle Literary and Dramatic Agency. Amy Lowell: 'Night Clouds' from *The Complete Poetical Works of Amy Lowell*. Copyright © 1955 by Houghton Mifflin Company. Reprinted by permission of Houghton Mifflin Company. Roger McGough: 'The Lesson' and 'First Day at School' from *In the Glassroom* and 'The Identification' from *Gig*. Reprinted by permission of Jonathan Cape Ltd. Mawther Maggie: 'A Mucky Job'. Reprinted by permission of the author. Merriam, Eve: 'Frying Pan' from *A Word or Two With You* copyright © 1981. 'Mean Song' from *There Is No Rhyme For Silver* copyright © 1962 by Eve Merriam. 'Teevee' from *Catch a Little Rhyme* copyright © 1966. Reprinted by permission of the author. Millay, Edna St. Vincent: 'Hearing your words and not a word among them' from *Collected Poems*, Harper and Row. Copyright 1931, 1958 by Edna St. Vincent Millay and Norma Millay Ellis. Spike Milligan: 'A Little Worm'. Reprinted by permission of Spike Milligan Productions Ltd. 'The Dog Lovers' from *Small Dreams of a Scorpion*. Reprinted by permission of Michael Joseph Ltd. Edwin Morgan: 'The Computer's First Christmas Card', 'Interference' and 'The First Men on Mercury' © Edwin Morgan, *Poems of Thirty Years*, Carcanet, Manchester 1982. Ogden Nash: 'The Pig' © Ogden Nash. Reproduced by permission of Curtis Brown Ltd., London. Grace Nichols: 'Granny Granny Please Comb My Hair' from *I Like That Stuff*, edited by M. Styles. Reprinted by permission of Cambridge University Press. 'Sea Timeless Song' from *The Fat Black Woman's Poems* by Grace Nichols, published by Virago Press Limited 1984. Copyright © Grace Nichols 1984. Norman Nicholson: 'Road Up' Norman Nicholson 1984/Reprinted from *The Candy-floss Tree*: poems by Gerda Mayer, Frank Flynn, and Norman Nicholson (1984) by permission of Oxford University Press. Leslie Norris: 'Boy Flying' from *Over the Bridge*. Reprinted by permission of the author. Frank Ormsby: 'Under the Stairs' © Frank Ormsby 1972. Reprinted from *A Store of Candles* by Frank Ormsby (1977) by permission of Oxford University Press. Jacques Prévert: 'The Eclipse', translated by Lawrence Ferlinghetti, from *Paroles*. Reprinted by permission of City Light Books. John Rice: 'Big Fears' from *Rockets and Quasars*. Reprinted by permission of the author. Alan Riddell: 'The Honey Pot' from *Eclipse*. Reprinted by permission of John Calder Publishers Ltd. Michael Rosen: 'Toothpaste' from *You Tell Me* by Roger McGough and Michael Rosen (Puffin Books 1981) pp. 62–63. Michael Rosen poems copyright © Michael Rosen 1979. This collection copyright © Penguin Books Ltd., 1979. Reprinted by permission of Penguin Books Ltd. Samih Al-Qasim: 'The Clock On the Wall' from *Victims of a Map*. Reprinted by permission of Al Saqi Books. Carl Sandburg: 'Manual System' from *Smoke and Steel* by Carl Sandburg, copyright 1920 by Harcourt Brace Jovanovich, Inc., renewed 1948 by Carl Sandburg. 'Elephants are Different to Different People' from *The Complete Poems of Carl Sandburg*, copyright 1950 by Carl Sandburg; renewed 1978 by Margaret Sandburg, Helga Sandburg Crile and Janet Sandburg. 'Gargoyle' from *Cornhuskers* by Carl Sandburg, copyright 1918 by Holt Rinehart and Winston, Inc., renewed 1946 by Carl Sandburg. 'Wars' from *Chicago Poems* by Carl Sandburg, copyright 1916 by Holt Rinehart and Winston, Inc., renewed 1944 by Carl Sandburg. 'from The People, Yes' from *The People, Yes* by Carl Sandburg, copyright 1936 by Harcourt Brace Jovanovich, Inc.; renewed 1964 by Carl Sandburg. Reprinted by permission of Harcourt Brace Jovanovich, Inc. Yetta Schmier: 'Weather' from *I Never Told Anybody* by Kenneth Koch. Copyright © 1977 by Kenneth Koch. Reprinted by permission of Kenneth Koch and Random House Inc. Ian Serraillier: 'Get Up and Shut the Door' and 'The Will' from *I'll Tell You a Tale* (Puffin Books) © 1973, 1976 Ian Serraillier and Puffin Books, England. 'The Diver' from *Happily Ever After* © 1963 Ian Serraillier and Oxford University Press. 'The Visitor' from *Oxford Second Poetry Book*, edited by J. Foster, © 1980 Ian Serraillier and Oxford University Press. Reprinted by permission of the author.

Robert Service: 'My Friends'. Reprinted by permission of Feinman and Krasilovsky. Tsuboi Shigeji: 'Silent, But . . .' from *The Penguin Book of Japanese Verse*, translated by Geoffrey Bownas and Anthony Thwaite (The Penguin Poets 1964) p. 191. Copyright © Geoffrey Bownas and Anthony Thwaite, 1964. Reprinted by permission of Penguin Books Ltd. Shel Silverstein: Text of 'Hungry Mungry' from *Where the Sidewalk Ends: the poems and drawings of Shel Silverstein*. Copyright © 1981 by Snake Eye Music Inc. 'Squishy Touch' and 'Kidnapped' from *A Light in the Attic*, by Shel Silverstein. Copyright © 1981 by Snake Eye Music, Inc. Reprinted by permission of Harper and Row Publishers Inc. and Jonathan Cape Ltd. Stevie Smith: 'Fairy Story' published in the UK in *The Collected Poems of Stevie Smith* (Allen Lane) and in the US by New Directions Publishing Corporation. Copyright 1972 by Stevie Smith. Reprinted by permission of James MacGibbon and New Directions Publishing Corporation. Sir John Squire: 'There Was an Indian' from *Verses Worth Remembering* by Sir John Squire. Reprinted by permission of Macmillan, London and Basingstoke. May Swenson: 'The Cloud-Mobile' by May Swenson, first printed in *A Cage of Spines*, copyright © 1958, is reprinted by permission of the author. D. M. Thomas: 'Moth'. Reprinted by permission of the author. J. R. R. Tolkien: 'The Mewlips' from *Adventures of Tom Bombadil* by J. R. R. Tolkien. Copyright © 1962 by George Allen and Unwin Ltd. 'This thing all things devours' from *The Hobbit*. Copyright © 1966 by J. R. R. Tolkien. Reprinted by permission of George Allen and Unwin Publishers Ltd. and Houghton Mifflin Company. Virgil: 'Mount Etna, A Volcano in Sicily' from *The Aeneid*, translated by C. D. Lewis. Reprinted by permission of the author's estate and Chatto and Windus. Margaret Walker: 'Lineage' from *For My People* (Yale University Press 1942). Reprinted by permission of the author. William S. Wallace: 'The Song of Snohomish'. Copyright © 1976 by the New York Times Company. Reprinted by permission. Colin West: 'When Betty Eats Spaghetti' from *Not to be Taken Seriously* by Colin West. Reprinted by permission of Hutchinson Publishing Group Ltd. William Carlos Williams: 'The Last Words of My English Grandmother 1920' and 'The Term' William Carlos Williams, *Collected Earlier Poems*. Copyright 1938 by New Directions Publishing Corporation. 'Suzanne' William Carlos Williams, *Collected Later Poems*. Copyright 1948 by William Carlos Williams. Reprinted by permission of New Directions Publishing Corporation. Judith Wright: 'Flood Year' published in the UK in *Judith Wright: Collected Poems 1942-1970* and in the US in *The Double Tree* by Judith Wright. Copyright © 1978 by Judith Wright. Reprinted by permission of Angus and Robertson (UK) Ltd. and Houghton Mifflin Company. Kit Wright: 'Sergeant Brown's Parrot' from *Rabbiting On* by Kit Wright. Reprinted by permission of Fontana Paperbacks.

Additional acknowledgements:
Bella Akhmadulina: 'Small Aircraft'. Reprinted by permission of Antaeus The Ecco Press. Eleanor Farjeon: 'Waking Up' from *Silver, Sand and Snow* (Michael Joseph Ltd.). Reprinted by permission of David Higham Associates Ltd. Cicely Herbert: 'Who'd Be A Juggler. Reprinted by permission of the author. Adrian Mitchell: 'Pause', 'Dumb Insolence' and 'Not a Very Cheerful Song I'm Afraid' from *Nothingmas Day* (1984) and 'Back in the Playground Blues' from *For Beauty Douglas* (1982). Vernon Scanell: 'A Case of Murder' from *Selected Poems* (1971). Reprinted by permission of Allison & Busby Ltd. Siv Widerberg: 'Stamps', 'Nightmare', and 'Papa' from *I'm Like Me* by Siv Widerberg (Old Westbury, N.Y. The Feminist Press, 1973). Original poems © 1968, 1970, 1971 by Siv Widerberg. Translations © 1973 by Verne Moberg. Reprinted with permission of The Feminist Press, Box 334, Old Westbury, New York 11568.

While every effort has been made to obtain permission, there may still be cases in which we have failed to trace a copyright holder, and we would like to apologize for any apparent negligence.

INDEX
Of Titles and First Lines

SUBJECT INDEX

(Please note: t=top (poem), m=middle, b=bottom.)

253

POETS

d'AGUIAR, Frederick (*b* 1960, Guyanese)
AHLBERG, Allan (*b* 1938, English)
AKHMADULINA, Bella (*b* 1937, Russian)
ALDIS, Dorothy (modern, English)
AL-KHANSA (*d* 645, Arab woman poet)
ANDREWS, Julie (modern, English)
AUDEN, Wystan Hugh (1907–73, Anglo/
American)
BABURKA, Ilona (modern, American)
BALLENTINE, Keith (modern, English)
BATCHELOR, John (modern, English)
BAYLY, Thomas Haynes (1797–1839,
English)
BELLOC, Hilaire (1870–1953, Anglo/French)
BENET, Stephen Vincent (1898–1943,
American)
BENTLEY, Edmund *Clerihew* (1875–1956,
English)
BETJEMAN, Sir John (1906–84, English)
BLAKE, William (1757–1827, English)
BRECHT, Bertolt (1898–1956, German)
BROWNING, Elizabeth Barrett (1806–61,
English)
BROWNJOHN, Alan (*b* 1931, English)
BYRON, Lord George (1788–1824,
English)
CAMPBELL, Ian (modern, Scottish)
CATULLUS (84–54 BC, Roman)
CAUSLEY, Charles (*b* 1917, English)
CHARLIP, Remy (modern, American)
CHAUCER, Geoffrey (1340–1400, English)
CHEEKS, Sharon (*b* 1972, English)
CHESTERTON, Gilbert Keith (1874–1936,
English)
CHÜ-I, Po (772–846, Chinese)
COLERIDGE, Mary Elizabeth (1861–1907,
English)
CRICHTON SMITH, Ian (*b* 1928,
Scottish)
CUMMINGS, Edward Estlin (1894–1962,
American)
DARLINGTON, Andrew (modern, English)
DAVIES, Idris (1905–53, Welsh)
DAVISON, Fiona (modern, English)
DEAN, Jan (modern, English)
DEKKER, Thomas (1572–1632, English)

DE LA MARE, Walter John (1875–1956,
English)
DICKINSON, Emily (1830–86, American)
DIGANCE, Richard (modern, English)
DONNE, John (1573–1631, English)
DOOLITTLE, Hilda (H.D.) (1886–1961,
American)
DRYDEN, John (1631–1700, English)
DYLAN, Bob (*b* 1941, American)
EASTLAKE, William (modern,
American)
ELIOT, Thomas Stearns (1888–1965,
Anglo-American)
EMERSON, Ralph Waldo (1803–82,
American)
ENRIGHT, Dennis Joseph (*b* 1920,
English)
ESPY, Willard J. (modern, American)
FARJEON, Eleanor (1881–1965, English)
FERLINGHETTI, Laurence (*b* 1919,
American)
FLINT, Francis Stewart (1885–1960,
English)
FLYNN, Frank (modern, English)
FROMAN, Robert (modern, American)
FROST, Robert Lee (1874–1963,
American)
GODDEN, James (modern, American)
HARDY, Thomas (1840–1928, English)
HEANEY, Seamus Justin (*b* 1939, Irish)
HEGLEY, James (modern, English)
HERBERT, Cicely (modern, English)
HERBERT, Sir Alan Patrick (1890–1971,
English)
HERRICK, Robert (1591–1674, English)
HOBERMAN, Mary Ann (modern,
American)
HOFFMANN, Dr Heinrich (1809–94,
German)
HOOD, Thomas (1799–1845, English)
HOSEGOOD, Lucy (modern, English)
HUGHES, James Langston (1902–67, Afro-
American)
HUGHES, Ted (*b* 1930, English, poet
laureate)
HURLEY, James (*b* 1933, English)

IBSEN, Henrik (1828–1906, Norwegian)
ISSAIA, Nana (b 1934, Greek)
JACKSON, David (modern, English)
JACKSON, Karen (modern, English)
de JÉSUS, Teresa (modern, Chilean)
JONSON, Ben (1573–1637, English)
KALHA, Deepak (modern, English)
KEATS, John (1795–1821, English)
KHE-THA-A-HI (Eagle Wing) (modern, American Indian)
KINGSLEY, Charles (1819–75, English)
KINSELLA, Thomas (b 1928, Irish)
KIPLING, Rudyard (1865–1936, English)
KIZER, Carolyn (modern, American)
LEAR, Edward (1812–88, English)
LENNON & McCARTNEY (1940–80 & b 1942, English)
LINDSAY, Nicholas Vachel (1879–1931, American)
LOGUE, Christopher (b 1926, English)
LONGFELLOW, Henry Wadsworth (1807–82, American)
LOWELL, Amy (1874–1925, American)
MACCOLL & SEEGER (modern, English & American)
MAGGIE, Mawther (Margaret E. Secker) (b 1937, English)
MARLOWE, Christopher (1564–93, English)
MCGOUGH, Roger (modern, English)
MERRIAM, Eve (modern, Afro-American)
MILLAY, Edna St Vincent (1892–1950, American)
MILLIGAN, Spike (b 1918, English)
MILTON, John (1608–74, English)
MITCHELL, Adrian (b 1932, English)
MONRO, Harold Edward (1879–1932, English)
MORGAN, Edwin (b 1920, Scottish)
von MORSTEIN, Petra (modern, German)
NASH, Ogden (1902–71, American)
NICHOLS, Grace (b 1950, Guyanese)
NICHOLSON, Norman (b 1914, English)
NORRIS, Leslie (modern, English)
O'NEILL, Oliver (modern, Irish)
ORMSBY, Frank (modern, English)
PEACOCK, Thomas Love (1785–1866, English)
POE, Edgar Allan (1809–49, American)
PRÉVERT, Jacques (1900–77, French)
PROUDLOCK, Geoffrey (b 1971, English)

RICE, John (modern, Scottish)
RIDDELL, Alan (modern, Scottish)
ROSEN, Michael (b 1946, English)
RÓŻEWICZ, Tadeusz (modern, Polish)
SAMIH AL-QASIM (b 1939, Arabic)
SAPPHO (c 600 BC, Greek, woman poet)
SANDBURG, Carl (1878–1967, American)
SCANNELL, Vernon (b 1922, English)
SCHMIER, Yetta (modern, American)
SEEKINGS, Valerie (modern, English)
SERRAILLIER, Ian (b 1912, English)
SERVICE, Robert (1874–1958, Canadian)
SHAKESPEARE, William (1564–1616, English)
SHELLEY, Percy Bysshe (1792–1822, English)
SILVERSTEIN, Shel (b 1932, American)
SMITH, Stevie (1902–71, English)
SNAPE, Wendy (modern, English)
SOUTHEY, Robert (1774–1843, English)
SQUIRE, Sir John Collings (1884–1958, English)
STEVENSON, Robert Louis (1850–94, Scottish)
SWENSON, May (modern, American)
TENNYSON, Alfred Lord (1809–92, English)
THOMAS, D. M. (b 1935, English)
TOLKIEN, John Ronald Reuel (1892–1973, English)
TOLSTOY, Leo (1828–1910, Russian)
TS'AO CHIH (192–232, Chinese)
UPWARD, Allen (modern, English)
VACCIANO, Troy (modern, American)
VIRGIL (70–19 BC, Roman)
WADE, John Stevens (modern, English)
WALKER, Margaret (b 1915, American)
WALLACE, William (b 1915, American)
WEST, Colin (modern, English)
WHITMAN, Walt (1819–92, American)
WHITTIER, John Greenleaf (1807–92, American)
WIDERBERG, Siv (modern, American)
WILLIAMS, China (modern, English)
WILLIAMS, William Carlos (1883–1963, American)
WRIGHT, Judith (b 1915, Australian)
WRIGHT, Kit (modern, English)
YEATS, William Butler (1865–1939, Irish)
YONGE, Gilbert V. (modern, English)
ZBIERSKI, Marie (modern, American)